trullo

Tim Siadatan

For Jordan

Foreword

There is a famous image by Piero della Francesca, *The Madonna of Mercy*, which I rather identify with. It depicts a benevolent figure with outstretched arms, gathering a little crowd in the folds of her cloak. You may not be surprised that I do not frequently associate myself with religious paintings, but this one strikes a chord: being a chef is somewhat like being a mother hen, nurturing, gathering people under your wing and remaining calm when everyone else is running around like headless chickens! Then there are those moments when you can cluck with pride when your chicks have fled the nest and take over their own coop. This painting reminds me of that, and being Italian it is all the more appropriate for Tim, for whom I feel immense mother-hen-ish pride.

But I cannot claim all the credit! This book reads as a history of Tim: Jamie Oliver, Moro, St. JOHN, we are all parents to our love child Tim and his cheeky grin. His pedigree is evident, yet the result is all his own. It is delightful. There is one dish at Trullo that I return to as often as I can: the pici cacio e pepe. It's my favourite and the dish sums up Tim's approach: a classic, but very much his. The slippery thick pasta, the oozy pepper sauce, the noodles giving you a cheesy whiplash on your glasses.

There is a wider history of Italian food in Britain into which Tim fits nicely. Let's step back in time. At around the moment that Franco Taruschio must have suffered some geographical confusion to have stepped off the train and found himself in Abergavenny, where he founded the seminal Walnut Tree, Elizabeth David was busy confusing the nation into thinking we should all be using Mediterranean ingredients. This is a controversial view, but I believe E. David to be responsible for a large number of disappointing tomato salads. Tomato salads are one thing in 1970s' Naples but quite another in 1970s' London, in November, with pale Sainsbury's tomatoes facing you wetly on your plate.

But all was not so bleak. Let me whisk you away to Soho, at the time a mass of Italian shops. Lina Stores and I Camisa still remain and they were always the core (an aside: it was very important to shop at either I Camisa or Lina Stores. You could not shop at both. Showing my open-mindedness, I used to shop at Lina, but have since moved to Camisa). On Saturdays my parents would take me in to Soho and the day could go one of two ways: either we would go shopping at one of these stores, or one of the many other Italian product shops that used to exist at the time, then return home and have a wonderful lunch of Italian goodies. Or the second choice was lunch at the Terrazza restaurant next to the French House, one of a new generation of restaurants, all crisp pink linen and chic, modern people ordering bottles of Corvo Bianco like there was no tomorrow. This was the life!

The next big moment in Britain's Italian lesson was Marcella Hazan. We had an Italian student lodging with us for a few months, the daughter of some architect friends of my father, and she brought my mother a copy of Marcella's Classic Italian Cookbook. I wonder if she had as much effect nationally is she did in my own household, where she single-handedly changed food as I knew it at home: how we thought about it, how we understood it. The Tomato Sauce III is still a firm family favourite all these years later – Margot and I always think that our children are made up of 90% pasta.

I am deeply envious of anyone who does Italian, as I have always wanted to, and eating Tim's food makes me dream of what might have been. There are some people – Georgio Locatelli, and Tim is another – who make pasta look simple. When I do it, it is never quite the same! Tim is a precise cook, but Italian food in the wrong hands suffers the danger of falling off the edge of rustic. You have to be very careful when you cook rustically, it can be mistaken for slapdash or a lack of care. These are not mistakes that Tim makes. He is subtle, precise, obsessive. My salad lesson seems to have made quite an impression upon him: a side salad is the touchstone of a kitchen. It is often forgotten then knocked together in a haphazard way, a lost object. A perfect salad, with perfectly dressed leaves, is a measure of how you cook everything else.

Let us return briefly to Elizabeth David and our sad tomatoes. We do not have to linger long on those tomatoes of old; fast forward some years and along came The River Café, bringing with it flavour, an emphasis on provenance and the celebration of the art of simple. The joy in a rabbit leg! The beauty of cabbage! Before The River Café it could have been a difficult thing to have an Italian restaurant in London, and care as deeply as Tim about the seasons. They are important to him, which is a good sign for an Italian chef, and this is very evident in his recipes. But it is a sensible understanding: he understands the limitations of being in London, not Naples. Enjoy the limitations, work with them! Enjoy what is available locally, supplemented with things that will travel well: cheeses, oils, tins, which give your dish the Italian boost rather than a sad Italian shadow.

I am reminded of a night out in Rome, with bright and glamorous young Italians. All they wanted to discuss, all night, was Puntarella (a Roman leaf). It struck me that it would be very odd to find such a thing in London: a group of young people discussing cabbage. Except perhaps in Tim's company – he would certainly be happy to discuss Roman leaves for hours.

Tim comes to dinner with me and Margot, and he and Margot have a jolly time together talking about cooking; their food philosophy is very similar. He is a sympathetic cook, which is a pleasure, and his pleasure in food is infectious. He is a warm soul, which is often the case with chefs, I find, but Tim particularly so. He has a knack of treating me, and those who come to his restaurants, like family. Speaking as a member of the extended family that has nurtured Tim over the years (and then returned to be nurtured by him), we are very proud step-parents.

trullo

1st June ~ Dinner

Salumi ~ Finocchiona and Salame Strolghino 7

Antipasti

Zucchini Fritti 4.5

Pappa al Pomodoro 4

Surf clams with tomato, parsley, chilli and garlic 7

Bruschetta with lardo, radish, caper berry, parsley 6

Asparagus Fonduta 7.5

Pasta

Pappardelle with rabbit ragu, orange and rosemary 5

Ravioli of girolle and ricotta 7.5

Charcoal grill

Salmon, samphire, sorrel and aioli 13.5

Roast suckling pig, borlotti beans, raddichio and salsa verde 12.5

Sea bass, Amalfi lemon and potato al forno, salsa rosso 12

Oven

Slow-cooked veal cheek in buttermilk, spring garlic, chipotli onion and swiss chard 15

Lentils, ricotta and wilted mixed greens 9

Dessert

Nespoli Sorbet 4

Salted caramel ice cream 5

Cherry and almond tart, creme fraiche 4.5

Cheese

Pecorino Il Fiorino (Semi-matured, Sheep) 7

Bosina Alta Langa (Cow, Sheep, Goat)

Gorgonzola Dolce Verde Carozzi (Cow)

Our meat comes from ethically treated animals, and our fish is from sustainable sources. Please ask you waiter for details.

SERVICE NOT INCLUDED

Introduction

One of my earliest memories as a child is of a busy kitchen in service. I'd perch under the pizza section at my Dad's restaurant on a sack of flour, sandwiched between trays of proving dough, scoffing buttery garlic bread while watching chefs' ankles scurrying around the kitchen. It seemed to me like the place where grown-ups played – albeit with lots of yelling and bad language – and I loved the speed and intense energy. I remember the sound of oven doors opening and slamming shut, wafts of pizza smacking me in the face and, as the night got busier, the 'ding, ding, ding, ding' of the service bell before the early-evening background hum of the restaurant turned into a roar of jolly eaters. From time to time, a pretty waitress would check on me, smiling and handing me a bottle of Coca-Cola with a straw or a banana split with a sparkler – pretty rock 'n' roll for a five-year-old. I didn't know it but the seed was planted and I was destined to be a chef.

Being in restaurant kitchens was one thing, but the penny really dropped when I was 13 on a family holiday in Le Marche. My mother had rented a farmhouse up in some sunflower fields and one day the farmer who owned the land came down in his little tractor with a glut of tomatoes. They were ginormous, pulsating; you know the ones, they sing to you. He gave them to us as a gift, along with some olive oil from his grove. Mum would make mid-afternoon snackettes and one day she just sliced tomatoes and left them in the sun for a little bit with some oil and salt. Me and my older brother were like, 'Mum, tomatoes, what the hell?!' But I remember eating them for the first time; they're still to this day one of the best things I've ever tasted. It was almost a spiritual moment. That was the beginning, those tomatoes; that was when I fell in love.

At 17, after coming back from travelling, I applied for Jamie Oliver's Fifteen, which was in its first year. I'd seen Jamie doing an interview on the regional news about the idea of setting Fifteen up; I just thought, 'who knows', and wrote a letter. I didn't think anything of it until I got a phone call a couple of weeks later and went for an interview; within four weeks, everything changed and I was fortunate enough to be chosen as one of the first trainees.

Fifteen was the catalyst for me becoming a professional chef. It opened my eyes to Italian food and the London restaurant scene. Jamie and the other chefs showed me the importance of cooking seasonally, using only the best produce, understanding its provenance – and most importantly, they taught me to cook! As everyone knows, Jamie is a remarkable man, and I was lucky to be able to work alongside him fairly often. His passion for Italian food and skill in the kitchen both made a huge impact on me as did his ambition, enthusiasm for life, ability to make shit happen and genuine interest in other human beings. He was a true inspiration back then when I was 18 and he continues to inspire me today.

While I was at Fifteen, my sous-chef Derek Dammann (one of the best chefs I've ever met) kept banging on about this restaurant called St. JOHN and how I had to go and eat this dish of roast bone marrow with parsley salad and toast. Eventually I went and sat at the bar; I remember feeling quite nervous but excited at the same time. A man in a pinstripe suit took my order and set me up with a crab pick and teaspoon; he asked if I'd eaten the dish before, explaining how you have to scoop the bone marrow out on to the toast, spreading it thickly and sprinkling it with wet sea salt before adding the salad on top, ensuring there was the correct ratio of parsley, shallot and caper in every bite. That first mouthful – god daaamn! The balance of fatty marrow married with capers, sharp raw shallot, earthy parsley and acidic lemon dressing, all riding on crunchy toasted sourdough – it was magic. I was instantly hooked and knew that I needed to work at this place and learn their skills . So I asked if could do work experience on my days off from Fifteen and thankfully they said yes.

I worked at St. JOHN on my days off until I finished Fifteen, then after graduating I did a stint in Sydney on a scholarship. I loved it, but when I got a phone call from St. JOHN saying there was a position coming up, I knew I had to come back to London and go for it – and fortunately I got the job. Something changed in me after my experience of being part of the St. JOHN team from 2003–2004. For sure my skill-set progressed and I became a far more competent, confident cook, but the culture of St. JOHN also changed my perspective on restaurants. Though there was a hierarchy in place, there was also equal respect for each person working; it taught me the value of teamwork.

While I was at St. JOHN, Fergus Henderson also taught me one of the most valuable lessons of my culinary life and something that really stuck with me. I was working on the 'garden' section (i.e. starters) and one of my responsibilities was a side salad. Fergus eloquently and eccentrically explained how I needed to put all of my attention and energy into nailing each salad I tossed, so that every customer noticed how even the simplest side could sing out. If I carried over that level of attention to detail into everything else I did as I progressed as a chef, he said, then it would serve me well. I share this lesson with chefs who are starting out – to be honest, it's a good analogy for life.

***

I first met Jordan through his cousin, a good friend of mine. He came round for dinner one night and we got on really well – and that was it. From then on, we started hanging out a lot. He used to have epic dinner parties at his house in Putney, and I would go and help him prep. They were quite famous, his dinners; he had one big, long table and they got pretty raucous. He loved cooking and I loved helping out and that's where our friendship started. When we became friends, Jordan was acting, but as he became more interested in food, he stopped and did a three-month cooking course at Leiths and started working in kitchens.

I had moved to Oxford and was working at the restaurant Q.I. where I became head chef at the ripe age of 23. I was having a nightmare trying to find people to work in the kitchen, so I called Jordan one day and said, 'look, I need help dude, fancy coming to help with a couple of shifts?' He ended up moving to Oxford and working in the kitchen with me, where he had the world's quickest promotion to sous-chef in the history of promotions! We worked together for a year and in that period talked about opening something together – the more we talked about it, the more we realised that we should do it, because there was something there. And so it began...

We returned to London keen to get going, but restaurants aren't the easiest things to set up – especially when you don't really know what you're doing. At first we had wanted to open a small pasta bar (exactly like our restaurant Padella in fact) as we both loved pasta and had realised that the only places in London where you could go to eat amazing pasta tended to be high-end restaurants. But after returning to the city, I went and worked at Moro and Jordan moved from the kitchen and started working front of house at the River Café, and we got even more into the restaurant side of things. We wanted to follow our hearts and open a proper restaurant first, partly to prove to ourselves that we could do it and make it work. Writing the business plan, raising money and finding a site all took longer than we thought though – and then the recession kicked in and that thwarted things further. But, we also weren't quite ready to open up our own place. It's funny how things work out; we learned so much from our years at Moro and the River Café, and Trullo wouldn't be the place it is now without that time.

In fact, all the restaurants Jordan and I worked at inspired us – and continue to inspire us – hugely. Though the food they serve may be different, what we learned from Fifteen, St. JOHN, Moro and the River Café is that all the chefs shared the same philosophy.

First: the importance of cooking according to the seasons, being sustainable, using amazing produce and really understanding where that produce comes from.

Second: really enjoying what you do and having fun. At Trullo, we care about food in the same way as our producers do, and that definitely translates both onto the plate and into the warm, buzzing energy of the restaurant.

Jordan and I both bring things to the table that are our own particular strengths and one of the reasons our partnership works so well is that we are clear on what those strengths are, even as, increasingly, they intertwine. He is my food partner for life. Everyone's got to have a food partner that they like going to restaurants with and enjoy eating with (who isn't your other half) – or I think you do, anyway – and Jordan is mine. Without him, none of this would be possible.

Looking back, Trullo was born of three things: the amazing places Jordan and I have worked, our enthusiasm and passion, and a lot of love and respect for each other. It's a restaurant built from family: for better or worse, we are like brothers. Alanna, Jordan's wife, was massively involved in setting up Trullo, and still is involved in the business. Family is what Trullo embodies now: we have a lot of key staff who have been with us for years and who definitely feel like extended family. When a restaurant is based on that, you're off to a strong start – it's a good recipe. I think people feel that in the restaurant – they feel comfortable and at ease, and it's no surprise that we get a lot of families coming in.

The restaurant

On 1st June 2010 we opened Trullo in Highbury in North London. It was a slow burner to get started – man, were we nervous. Our aim was to create an Italian-inspired neighbourhood restaurant where the quality of food and service was up there with the best, without being prohibitively expensive – we wanted our demographic to be anyone.

I always wanted an open kitchen. Jordan and I looked at some good sites where that wasn't possible, but I was adamant. One reason was that being a chef and not seeing daylight is miserable and, I think, unfair and counterproductive. Unless it's an absolute necessity, I would avoid it at all costs. But the main reason was for customers to have that element of interaction. Not directly seeing what's going on in the kitchen, but knowing that it's happening, adds a different feeling to a restaurant. It is part of the theatre of the whole thing, and brings people together. Whether the kitchen is in people's peripheral vision or not, it creates an atmosphere. Trullo was always going to be loud and have a hustle and bustle to it, and I like the aromas and charcoal smell that come out of our kitchen. We always wanted the aesthetic to be simple, warm and comforting. The big windows bringing in all that natural light were a bonus. We realised that we didn't have to play around with the set-up too much, though we had our friend Lisa help us with the design; I'd be blagging if I said it was my vision!

When I was writing the first Trullo menu it was June; I remember thinking that I was really happy we'd opened at that time of year, because there was so much beautiful produce around. They were a hot few days, and I was able to write a really lovely light summer menu.

Our focus was mostly on regional Italian food initially – quite safe and classic – and I was surprised when I started creating my own dishes and got good feedback from customers. I realised then that I should start playing around more. This is the thing about confidence in cooking, and I hope I communicate it in this book: the more you play with stuff, the more confident you become. Everyone has it in them; you've just got to start believing in yourself a little bit more. At first, I didn't know I had it in me to do that. I probably went a bit too off piste at times – for all the good recipes I've come up with, there's the same amount of stuff that's not worked out. But that's part and parcel of the process. Don't be afraid of mucking up because if you don't try then you're never going to find out whether it's good or not. The way the menu is structured – antipasti, primi, pasta, grill, oven – has never changed but it wasn't until about six months in that Trullo started to develop into what it has become.

Trullo has changed massively over the years. We started with the restaurant on the ground floor and opened just in the evenings, Monday-Saturday. Then, after a while, we opened up the basement, where we served little tapas-style sharing plates, which worked but was too much – essentially we were running two restaurants on two floors and it was so busy that we were stretched thin. So we refurbished the basement and changed it completely and reopened serving the same menu on both floors. It's a lot less stressful now, even though we do more covers, and the only time we close is Sunday evening.

Wanting to have a neighbourhood restaurant is one thing. But for the first year, it was crazy; we were fully booked for a long time, months in advance, and people were travelling to visit. Years later, we actually are a neighbourhood restaurant. People do still travel from all over to eat at Trullo but we have a core percentage of customers who are locals and who come all the time. We know them, and they're on first name terms with us. Trullo is embedded into Highbury Corner now. Our regular customers are integral: the bread and butter of our business, the reason we set it up, and our community. They are as much a part of Trullo as the staff who have been with us for a long time. One regular, in his early eighties, would come in 3–4 times a week by himself for lunch. He'd sit at table five with a newspaper and would always have a little snooze up against the pillar after eating. When he later passed away, we were all really affected by it, because we used to see him all the time, and he was a lovely man. We asked his family if we could put up a little photo of him. There are lots of people like that. We're very proud of the fact that, for a lot of people, Trullo is the place they go on a regular basis, for their happy time; often they've become friends.

The Book

The recipes in this book include some of our favourite Italian classics, but the majority are my creations, trialled and tested on the menu at Trullo over the years.

This book is about serious cooking but without the seriousness. It's not difficult, and on the whole, it's not particularly time-consuming – it's just about attention to detail and taking note of the easy techniques that maximise flavour, or create unctuous, silky pasta sauces.

I've written these recipes for the home cook, to show that you can create luxurious, show-stopping feasts – like a slow-braised lamb shoulder cooked with peas, potatoes and mint in just one tray – that will not only have you jumping from foot to foot as they come out of the oven, but that require a minimum of prep work and washing up. And you can still feel like you're eating food in a proper Italian trattoria without splashing out: a simple plate of Tuscan pici (made from just flour and water) is as frugal – and delicious – as it gets.

Kitchen equipment

When I talk to people about cooking and they ask my advice on what to invest in, I tend to start with the basics. Pots and pans: you can't cook properly without good ones. So, what are your pans like? Because often they're crap – they're thin, they don't conduct heat evenly, the enamel has gone causing food to stick, or (a pet hate) they have plastic handles. Crap pans will stitch you up when it comes to trying to cook a great meal.

You need good tools to be able to create something exceptional. Knives are so varied; you can buy a Victorinox for twenty quid or a Japanese knife for £1000. As long as you look after your knife, it's going to stay sharp, and that is the most important thing. Quality pans aren't the cheapest of items, but if you buy one really good pot, a non-stick frying pan, a casserole dish and a roasting tray then they will look after you – much more so than an amazing knife. I promise they make a world of difference. Treat them right and they will last you a lifetime.

Fridge and store cupboard staples

If you want to cook from this book regularly (and even if you don't!) I highly recommend that you have invest in the list of ingredients opposite. They all have a decent shelf life and are versatile, useful ingredients that will help with the recipes here – and just generally in your cooking life!

Fridge: salsa rossa (page 239); anchovy paste (page 240); purple olives; salted ricotta; bottarga; salted anchovies; salted capers; cornichons; gorgonzola dolce; parmesan; Dijon mustard; pancetta; nduja; Marsala; chicken stock (page 245).

Dry store: whole dried chillies; Cabernet Sauvignon vinegar; Moscatel vinegar; good-quality extra virgin olive oil; wild, dried, bunched oregano; Castelluccio lentils; dried chickpeas; dried borlotti beans; dried cannellini beans; real polenta (not the three-minute sort!); dried pasta (De Cecco is affordable and good).

OLIO EXTRA VERGINE
DI OLIVA

Prodotto ed imbottigliato da Azienda Agricola

CHIARENTANA
di Donata Origo
Loc Chiarentana - Chianciano Terme SI Italia
info@chiarentanaolio.com
www.chiarentanaolio.com

Olio di Oliva di Categoria Superiore
ottenuto direttamente dalle olive
unicamente mediante procedimenti meccanici

RACCOLTO 2016

CHIARENTANA

Contenuto ml 5000 ℮

ORIGINE ITALIANA

Lotto

30/06/16

A note on olive oil

Olive oil is a seasoning, an integral part of lots of Italian cooking, and needs to be respected. Just like grapes, there are hundreds of varieties of olives with their own unique character that produce different kinds of oil. And just like wine, olive oil quality can vary massively. Often huge companies buy olives from all over the place, have little respect for them and use bogus methods to extract every millilitre of oil without giving a monkey's about the end product. Most of these oils are stocked in supermarkets with strong branding, but trust me, they're poor to average and if you want to up your cooking game, don't buy them! In Italy, the people who dedicate their lives to producing the finest wines often transfer that passion and professionalism into producing the finest olive oil; the big difference is that the price of a bottle of their wine can spiral into three figures (which, once opened, needs to be drunk then or very soon after). But the finest olive oil will cost between £15–£30; you only use a bit at a time and, unlike wine, it will last for a few months once opened, if stored correctly. It's a sound investment and one I urge you to make. Remember, every time I say to use olive oil in this book, I mean the real deal! (Use a rubber wine stopper and a pump to withdraw the oxygen and it will help keep the quality for longer.)

Olive oil is pressed around late autumn; like all fruits, olives are at their peak the moment they are picked. So, freshly pressed new season olive oil is the best and, although the quality deteriorates, it's still good (if sealed) for a year until the next harvest. When buying, check the label for the most recent bottling date.

Conscious eating

We're extremely fortunate to be able to have almost any food product we desire delivered to our door. But with this outrageously fortuitous position comes a responsibility to source and eat consciously: it's vital we mix up our diet so we don't unnecessarily fly produce across the world or see species wiped to near-extinction. Consider too that when it comes to branding animal products, the vaguer the description, the more likely it is that the animal welfare is poor. 'Pork from British farms' and a Union Jack on the package will nearly always mean miserable pigs from somewhere in the UK. If you're not sure and want to know, always ask the question.

Chapter 1:
Antipasti

Antipasti

When I was a kid, my gorgeous Ma first introduced me to the idea of antipasti, except that, being English, she called them 'snackettes'. Whether we were on holiday or on weekends, or just after hours of running around playing, she would often produce a tray of pit-stop goodies to refuel us until supper.

When, years later, I first started eating in Italy, I soon realised that seasonal antipasti is pretty much everywhere there. Go to a hole in the wall for a spritz and you get served a mixed plate of olives, breadsticks and cured meats. Hang out in a trattoria, order from the counter and get a selection of crostinis, marinated anchovies and arancini. Eat at an agriturismo and an Italian mamma will bring out a selection of seasonal home-grown wilted greens tossed in olive oil from their grove, chopped chicken liver and fresh focaccia and, if you're lucky, fresh cheese made from their goats. Basically, antipasti is a style of grazing that can be the start of a big feast (and the catalyst to good times) or simply something to fill rumbling tummies between meals while having a glass or two.

At Trullo, we always recommend the idea of sharing antipasti but in England people often have it as an individual starter or singularly as a light lunch – do whatever floats your boat.

Pot-roast Brussels sprouts, crispy pancetta, chestnut and gorgonzola fonduta

Brussels sprouts have a bad rep in the UK, as we tend only to cook them as part of Christmas dinner where they're often neglected and become a nostalgic nuisance. But, while this recipe uses traditional sprout-friendly ingredients like pancetta and chestnuts, it brings the misunderstood dwarf cabbage to the fore and allows it to have centre stage.

Serves 4

2–3 rashers pancetta
2–3 cooked chestnuts
20g unsalted butter
a splash of olive oil
880g Brussels sprouts (220g per person), washed and roots trimmed
a good glug of Marsala
450ml chicken stock (see page 245)
3 heaped tablespoons gorgonzola dolce
1 tablespoon crème fraîche
a small handful of chopped parsley
salt and black pepper

Heat your grill to high, or put a frying pan on a medium to high heat. Grill or fry the pancetta until crisp then remove and leave on a metal rack to cool and crisp further. Break up into small sprinkly bits.

Coarsely chop the chestnuts into little pieces and fry in butter on a low heat until crispy. Drain on kitchen paper.

Heat a splash of olive oil in a pan on a medium to low heat and fry the Brussels sprouts until golden. Add some Marsala and reduce for a minute. Add enough chicken stock to cover the Brussels by three-quarters, and season with salt and pepper. Cover with a lid and cook on a low to medium heat for about 12 minutes; you want the sprouts to be soft but not squidgy.

While the sprouts are cooking, heat the gorgonzola dolce and crème fraîche together in a pan over a very low heat, stirring occasionally, until the gorgonzola melts and they become one in a smooth, creamy fonduta.

Place the Brussels sprouts on hot plates and gloss with the cooking liquid; pour the fonduta all over and sprinkle over the chestnuts, pancetta and parsley.

Seared chicken liver, raspberry, frisée and chive salad with mustard dressing

This makes a perfect starter or light lunch on a warm summer's day when raspberries are in season and singing.

The recipe makes a large quantity of dressing, but you can keep it in the fridge for five days. Use it on salad, or get more creative and mix it through mashed potato, stir it through chopped leeks to make leeks vinaigrette, or spoon it over chicken before roasting for a nice mustardy crust.

Serves 2

1 whole frisée, washed
16 fresh raspberries
1 tablespoon finely chopped chives
a splash of olive oil
10 chicken livers (ask your butcher to remove any sinew)

For the dressing (makes about 450ml)
2 tablespoons Dijon mustard
300ml olive oil
½ tablespoon red wine vinegar
¼ garlic clove, minced
salt and pepper

First make the dressing. Put the Dijon mustard in a mixing bowl and slowly whisk in the olive oil until it emulsifies. Add the vinegar and garlic and season with salt and pepper to taste.

Heat a frying pan on a medium heat.

Tear the frisée into roughly 4cm strips and put in a separate mixing bowl along with the raspberries and chives.

Add a touch of olive oil to the hot frying pan, followed by the livers. Sear them on one side for 1½ minutes, then turn over and sear the other side for 1 minute. Remove from the pan to a plate and leave to stand for 60 seconds, then slice each liver into three pieces.

Mix the salad with the warm livers and some dressing. Serve immediately.

Sea bass carpaccio with blood orange and fennel

Clean, healthy, tasty and so pretty!

Serves 2

1 blood orange
100g super-fresh sea bass (ideally wild), filleted and pin-boned
a glug of olive oil
4 sprigs of fennel tops, picked (alternatively, a small sprinkle of
    toasted and pounded fennel seeds would work)
salt

You will need to prepare 8 segments of orange. Top and tail the orange on a chopping board. Sit it on its tail and, with a sharp knife, cut off the rind and pith. You will see the natural divides of the segments. Working over a bowl in order to catch the juice, cut in between these divides: what will slot out will be little wedges of orange.

Slice the sea bass fillets on an angle so that you end up with pieces of sea bass around 4cm long and 1cm thick. Lay them out on a plate and sprinkle with salt. Leave for a couple of minutes for the salt to react with the fish – as in curing, the salt reacts with the protein and starts to take the moisture out, tenderising the flesh, making the texture a little smoother and giving you better flavour.

Fill in the gaps on the plate with orange segments. Pour any orange juice from the bowl on the fish and drizzle the whole dish with olive oil. Garnish with fennel tops.

Steamed asparagus with chopped egg yolk, cornichon, caper, tarragon and chervil

Asparagus comes back into our lives around late spring, and at Trullo we tend to have a variety of asparagus recipes on the menu. We gorge on the fat, juicy emerald spears for the six or so weeks they're around and then leave them be until next year. If asparagus isn't in season you could use leeks here instead.

Do buy salt-packed capers: the brined ones taste too vinegary. To desalinate, simply rinse the capers and leave them in a bowl of water for an hour or two, changing the water a couple of times. Moscatel vinegar is sweet and quite subtle, it works well as a gentle acid background – I find other vinegars too strong for this dish.

Serves 2

2 large free-range or organic eggs (at room temperature)
1 tablespoon finely chopped tarragon leaves
1 tablespoon finely chopped flat-leaf parsley leaves
8 sprigs of chervil, picked
1 teaspoon capers, desalinated and finely chopped
1 tablespoon cornichons, roughly chopped
a splash of Moscatel vinegar
a glug of olive oil
14 asparagus spears, or 10 baby leeks or 2 leeks
salt and black pepper

Boil the eggs for 9 minutes, then leave to cool and peel. Cut each in half and discard half of the egg white. Roughly chop the yolks with the remaining whites, and put in a bowl. Add the herbs, capers, cornichons, vinegar and olive oil. Mix thoroughly and season with salt and pepper.

Trim the asparagus and discard any woody stalks. Boil in lightly salted water for 3 minutes and drain.

Line the asparagus on a plate like soldiers and spoon the egg mixture in a thick line across the middle.

Burrata with smashed broad beans, anchovy and chilli

Simple and sexy, this is best when made with the smaller broad beans you get at the beginning of summer.

It's important to use really good-quality salted anchovies – I like the Ortiz brand. If you want to, use whole anchovies; to debone them, first pull off the head, then hold on to the spine and in one motion pull the bone away.

Serves 2

100g broad beans, podded
4 anchovy fillets, or 2 salted whole anchovies
100ml olive oil
½ teaspoon finely chopped deseeded dried chilli
1 teaspoon finely grated lemon zest
juice of ¼ lemon
2 x 120g burrata (you could also use good-quality buffalo mozzarella)
salt

Boil the broad beans in lightly salted water for 1 minute, then drain and put in iced water to stop the cooking process, then drain immediately.

Slice the anchovy fillets into whiskers.

With a pestle and mortar, smash the broad beans with a tiny sprinkle of salt so they break up coarsely. Add the olive oil, chilli, lemon zest, juice and the anchovy whiskers, and stir together. Leave for 10 minutes to macerate.

Tear the burrata on to plates and spoon the broad bean mix over the top.

Baccalà and green tomato with oregano and Cabernet Sauvignon vinegar dressing

The sweetness of this dressing against the sharp tomato and creamy salt cod is a frisky combination.

The baccalà (dried, salted cod) lasts for 3–5 days in the fridge and is good to have around, so I recommend making a slightly bigger batch than required. I like any leftovers on hot toast, stirred into pasta, mixed into beans with a splash of water then blitzed slightly to make soup, packed into courgette flowers and steamed, spread in a sandwich with sliced soft boiled egg and watercress, or with crispy pancetta for a breakfast sandwich... The possibilities are endless!

Serves 2

a drizzle of olive oil
1 teaspoon Cabernet Sauvignon vinegar
a sprinkle of dried oregano
2 tomatoes, ideally green for a sharper flavour

For the baccalà
300ml olive oil
300g desalinated salt cod
4 bay leaves
3 garlic cloves, roughly chopped
juice of ½ lemon
salt and black pepper

First make the baccalà. In a saucepan large enough to hold the salt cod, heat the olive oil on a low heat. Add the bay leaves and chopped garlic, and fry for 20 minutes until soft. Discard the bay leaves, turn the heat to medium, add the salt cod and cook for 5 minutes more until the cod breaks up.

Strain the cod through a sieve or colander with a bowl underneath to catch the cod-infused oil. Transfer the cod to a food processor and whizz for a minute. Start to incorporate the cod-infused oil in a steady thin stream until the cod becomes a thick paste (not runny). Add the lemon juice, and a good grind of black pepper and salt to taste (how much you need will depend on how salty your cod is).

To make the dressing, whisk together a drizzle of olive oil, Cabernet Sauvignon vinegar and oregano. Slice the green tomatoes into 2cm rounds and lay on a plate. Drizzle with the dressing and spoon baccalà on top of each slice.

Grilled ox heart, baked borlotti beans and salsa rossa

A Trullo classic, much loved by our customers and one of our most popular dishes. If your butcher doesn't stock ox heart, they can easily order it for you.

Serves 4

200g ox heart (ask your butcher to remove any arteries and sinew)
280g fresh borlotti beans, podded, or dried (soaked in water overnight if dried)
2 garlic cloves
3 bay leaves
2 sprigs of rosemary
a glug of olive oil
1 ripe tomato (any kind)
salsa rossa (see page 239)

Make the salsa rossa from the recipe on page 239.

Put the borlotti beans in a pan and add the garlic, bay, rosemary and a glug of olive oil, and cover with water. Squash the tomato in your hands, add it to the pan and cook on a low to medium heat for 30 minutes, or until tender (if you are using dried beans this may take up to 15–30 minutes longer).

While the beans are cooking, place the ox heart on a chopping board and with a sharp knife slice into 5cm strips, 1–2cm thick.

Remove a quarter of the beans from the pan and whizz them into a paste with a stick blender or in a food processor, then add them back to the whole beans.

Preheat a Bbq or griddle pan to hot. When it is hot, spoon the warm beans on to plates. Season the ox heart with salt and pepper, grill on one side for 1 minute, then turn and cook for 30 seconds more.

Serve immediately on top of the beans, and drizzle over some salsa rossa.

Roast sticky salsify, glazed cipollini onion and gorgonzola fonduta

Salsify is available over the colder months of the year, and this dish is perfect for a cold winter's night. Salsify is a weird, bark-y little vegetable and doesn't taste like you might imagine (you wouldn't expect it to be pale white when you peel it). It has a high sugar content so it gets quite sticky and when you cook it, it turns from being quite savoury to quite sweet. Salsify oxidises very quickly so as soon as you have peeled it, leave it to sit in water with some lemon juice to stop it discolouring.

Serves 2

4 cipollini onions or shallots, peeled
2 garlic cloves, peeled
olive oil
2 salsify, washed and peeled and cut into 10cm batons
200ml chicken or vegetable stock (see pages 244–245)
2 tablespoons gorgonzola dolce
½ tablespoon crème fraîche
flat-leaf parsley, finely chopped, to garnish
salt and pepper

Preheat the oven to 180°C/gas mark 4.

Put the cipollini onions or shallots in a roasting tray, then add the garlic, a glug of olive oil, some salt and pepper and a splash of water, and cover tightly with foil. Roast for 1 hour 30 minutes, checking from time to time to stir. If the onions are catching on the pan, add a splash more water and shake the tray.

While they are roasting, heat some olive oil in a pan large enough to hold all the salsify on a medium to low heat. Working in batches so that you don't have more than one layer, start to colour the salsify until golden. Once all the salsify is done put them all back into the pan, add the stock and bring to a simmer, then simmer for about 10 minutes, covered, until just soft. Season with salt and pepper.

When everything is ready and still hot, heat the gorgonzola dolce and crème fraîche over a low heat until the gorgonzola has melted and all has combined into a creamy fonduta. Place the salsify and cipollini onions or shallots evenly across a plate and drizzle with fonduta, then sprinkle chopped parsley over to garnish.

Bocconcini with grilled marinated radicchio

This a perfect, simple starter for a dinner party: bocconcini are bite-sized mozzarella balls (alternatively, you can tear up a bigger piece of mozzarella), and the radicchio can be prepared up to three days ahead. Just lay everything out on a serving platter for everyone to help themselves. Or you could toast a slice of bread to make a quick but indulgent lunch.

The radicchio tastes amazing when grilled on a charcoal Bbq – if you don't have one, or don't want the hassle, you can use a griddle pan.

Serves 2

½ radicchio, washed
olive oil
grated zest and juice of ½ orange
½ teaspoon caster sugar
1 teaspoon dried oregano
a splash of Cabernet Sauvignon vinegar
8–10 bocconcini
salt

Preheat the Bbq or griddle pan on a medium heat (make sure the griddle is clean), and preheat the oven to 180°C/gas mark 6.

Cut the radicchio into quarters with the root still on to hold the leaves together. Rub or brush the cut sides with olive oil and place on the grill. Leave for 2 minutes then turn over and leave for 2 minutes more. Transfer to a roasting tray and add the orange zest and juice, caster sugar, oregano, a glug of olive oil, a splash of water and the vinegar and salt to taste. Cover tightly with foil and bake for 20 minutes. Remove from the oven and leave to cool but leave the foil tightly sealed to finish the cooking process.

Serve at room temperature next to the balls of bocconcini.

Castelfranco, blood orange, pomegranate, mint and ubriaco salad

Every year when blood oranges come into season around January, this salad instantly goes on the menu at Trullo, bringing a sparkle to the winter gloom. If you can't find Castelfranco, you could use ordinary radicchio instead. Ubriaco is know as 'drunken' cheese because it's matured in the skins of grapes that have been pressed for wine.

Serves 2

½ Castelfranco, washed and torn into large pieces
12 segments of blood orange (see page 28)
1 tablespoon pomegranate seeds
6 mint leaves, finely chopped
a splash of Cabernet Sauvignon vinegar
a splash of olive oil
ubriaco or pecorino cheese, finely grated
salt

Put all the ingredients except the ubriaco or pecorino in a large bowl, add a bit of salt and gently mix together. Evenly distribute on plates and sprinkle the cheese on top.

Pink grapefruit, lamb's lettuce and salted ricotta

This takes minutes to assemble but has maximum impact.

Serves 2

½ pink grapefruit, segmented (see page 28) and each segment cut
  in half
3 handfuls lamb's lettuce
a splash of Cabernet Sauvignon vinegar
a splash of olive oil
4 tablespoons coarsely grated salted ricotta cheese
salt

Put all the ingredients except the salted ricotta in a mixing bowl and toss together. Season with a pinch of salt. Distribute evenly on plates and sprinkle the salted ricotta on top.

Agretti, new season olive oil and lemon

Agretti (monk's beard) grows around southern Europe and is in season from February to April. It has a wonderful mineral-y flavour. I adore this super-simple combination of peppery olive oil and citrus and could eat it by the bucket load, but agretti is also amazing with garlic butter or fried chilli, garlic and anchovy; tossed together with dressed crab or with spicy tomato sauce (see page 107); deep-fried in tempura; and slow-cooked with whole lamb shoulder.

Serves 2

2 bunches agretti (washed and trimmed at the base)
a glug of new season olive oil
juice of ½ lemon
salt and pepper

Bring a large pot of water to the boil, add a pinch of salt and drop in the agretti, then simmer for 2–3 minutes. Drain and chill in iced water to stop the cooking process. Take out as soon as it's chilled and drain again.

Put some olive oil into a pan, add the lemon juice and drained agretti, season with salt and pepper and toss on a medium heat for a minute or so, then serve.

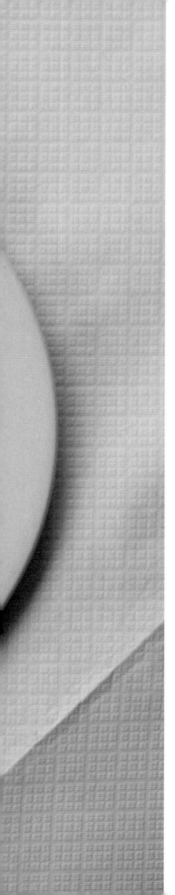

Bruschetta

Bruschetta is a versatile little number. It can be whatever you need it to be: a quick lunch, late afternoon snackette, hearty supper, starter for a dinner party, midnight munchie, or easy-to-assemble canapé. There's no real British equivalent to bruschetta – when you go to a gastropub or a hotel you get mushrooms on toast, or there's beans on toast, of course, but it's a different vibe.

Crostini is bite-sized and eaten with your fingers (when you're having an aperitivo, say) but bruschetta is bigger – more of a starter, and something that you would eat with a knife and fork. The ideal for bruschetta is a slice of bread 15cm long by 8cm wide: that is a solid size; a meal!

At Trullo we use our own sourdough bread, but you can use whatever floats your boat, though ideally you want bread that toasts well and has structural integrity. You don't have to use fresh bread when making bruschetta; you don't want it to be stale and dried out, but if it is a few days old then it will toast a little better.

We use our charcoal grill to toast the bread, which adds an extra layer of flavour. Lighting a Bbq to toast some bread might seem a tad excessive when cooking at home, so a griddle pan, grill or toaster will do the job nicely.

As with almost all cooking in Italy, bruschetta toppings vary according to the season. At Trullo in spring I'll often use cod's roe to make a spread: gently heat in a frying pan or a roasting tray with a tiny bit of water and butter on a low, low heat for about 5 minutes until warmed through and just cooked. Split them, take the roe out and place in a bowl. Start emulsifying by whisking with olive oil, then add lemon juice, salt and pepper, and you have a lovely paste for your toast. This is a good base for a lot of spring things: put raw peas on top, asparagus, agretti, samphire, artichokes, spinach, soft-boiled eggs…

Here are some other ideas for bruschetta combinations.

Spring

1. Ricotta and fresh peas
2. Brown crab and agretti
3. Pancetta, clams and wild garlic
4. Chopped asparagus, brown shrimp, lemon and olive oil

Summer

1. San Marzano tomato and oregano
2. Slow-cooked green and yellow courgette and mint
3. Burrata, summer peas and sorrel
4. Tomato and white crab

Autumn

1. Smashed pumpkin, confit garlic and ricotta
2. Chicken liver and grilled fig
3. Braised game and Chianti with new season olive oil
4. Chopped wild mushrooms, garlic and parsley

Winter

1. Lardo, anchovy and sliced shallot
2. Slow-cooked cime di rapa (or sprouting broccoli)
   and new season olive oil
3. Mozzarella and purple olives
4. Cabbage and steamed mussels

Braised cuttlefish, dried porcini, thyme and Marsala with bone marrow bruschetta

One of the great joys of cooking is that sometimes there is no rhyme or reason to why certain flavour combinations work, but when it happens, it's time to do the funky chicken!

Cuttlefish is a meatier, more robust version of squid. When you cook it low and slow it has a wonderful buttery texture.

For a meat-free alternative to the bone marrow, you could roast some tomatoes with a splash of olive oil in an oven preheated to 200°C/gas mark 6 (about 25 minutes for small cherry tomatoes) until they are totally blistered and juicy. Add a splash of water partway through cooking if you think they need it. Smudge them on top of the toast, along with all the juice and olive oil. Really get it saturated so that when you cut into it you get that nice tomato-flavoured bread.

Serves 2

2 veal marrow bones, cut into roughly 7cm pieces (you might have to
    order these from your butcher)
2 tablespoons dried porcini mushrooms
olive oil
1 onion, peeled and finely sliced
1 garlic clove, peeled, plus another cut clove to rub
4 sprigs of thyme and 4 bay leaves, tied together with string
700g cleaned cuttlefish (ask your fishmonger to do this for you)
25ml Marsala
175ml water
a squeeze of lemon juice
8 leaves of parsley, finely chopped
2 decent slices of good toasting bread, such as sourdough
salt and pepper

Preheat the oven to 200°C/gas mark 6. Roast the marrow bones for 25 minutes, then take out of the oven and allow to cool. Scoop out the marrow with a teaspoon and chill in the fridge. It will keep for up to 3 days.

Preheat the oven to 180°C/gas mark 4. Rinse the porcini to get rid of any dust. Put in a pan with 200ml water and bring to the boil, then reduce the heat and simmer for 10 minutes.

Meanwhile, heat a splash of olive oil in a frying pan on a low to medium heat. Add the onion and cook gently for 20 minutes until starting to colour, then add the garlic, thyme and bay leaves and fry for 5 minutes until golden. Transfer to a roasting tray or casserole dish and add the cuttlefish, porcini and their stock, Marsala, water, some olive oil, salt and pepper, and stir. Cover tightly with foil or a lid and braise in the oven for 1 hour 20 minutes. The cuttlefish should be soft and tender. Check the seasoning then fold in the lemon juice and parsley.

Heat the bone marrow until soft. Toast the bread, rub with a cut clove of raw garlic, spoon on melted bone marrow and sprinkle with salt. Spoon the hot cuttlefish on top.

Burrata and anchovy

Life is always better with anchovy paste in your fridge, and this bruschetta is
even better with a ball of burrata on top.

Serves 2

1 tablespoon anchovy paste (see page 240)
1 ball of burrata
2 slices of bread
salt

Toast the bread. Spread with a thick layer of anchovy paste, place the burrata
on top and sprinkle with salt.

Rabbit offal

If you are scared of offal, then this is quite a mild-tasting entry point and worth giving a go. Devilled kidneys on toast can be quite pungent but this is delicate, mild and subtle. It is really good for brunch – especially with a fried egg.

If your butcher doesn't stock rabbit offal, they will be able to order it for you.

Serves 2

6 rabbit hearts, 4 livers and 6 kidneys
a splash of olive oil
2 slices of bread
4 sage leaves
50ml Marsala
50ml chicken stock (see page 245)
20g unsalted butter
salt and pepper

Cut away any stringy sinew surrounding the offal (if you're not confident doing this, ask your butcher to do it for you) and discard.

Heat some olive oil in a frying pan on a high heat. Put the bread on to toast, then season the offal with sage and salt and add to the frying pan. Leave the offal to colour on one side for 1½ minutes then turn the pieces over and add the Marsala. Cook for 30 seconds, then add the chicken stock, the butter and some pepper and reduce for 1 minute. Serve the offal and gravy on top of the toast.

Sardine, nduja, Datterini tomato, oregano and lemon

This calls for the freshest ingredients: sardines with rigor, tomatoes that sing and nobbly unwaxed lemons. Fresh anchovies are also really good with this.

Serves 2

16 Datterini tomatoes (or ripe cherry tomatoes)
a few splashes of olive oil
a dash of Cabernet Sauvignon vinegar
1 tablespoon nduja
12–16 sardines(depending on their size), butterflied and
    spine removed, or 16–24 fresh anchovies
1 teaspoon dried oregano
2 slices of bread
grated zest of ¼ lemon, plus lemon wedges, to serve
1 tablespoon finely chopped curly parsley
salt

Roughly chop the tomatoes and put in a bowl. Add a sprinkle of salt, a splash of olive oil and a tiny dash of vinegar then leave to macerate.

Preheat grill on the highest heat.

Put the nduja into a bowl, add 20ml of hot water and a splash of olive oil, and whisk into a loose paste. Smother the paste over the sardines or anchovies and sprinkle with oregano and salt. Lay out on a grill tray and grill for 2 minutes.

Toast the bread. Squidge the tomatoes and their oil into the toast, lay the sardines or anchovies over and spoon some nduja mix on top. Finish with finely grated lemon zest and chopped parsley and serve with a lemon wedge.

Mushyish peas

Inspired by good old Blighty fish and chip dinners, these peas are cooked the Trullo way. They are also good as a garnish with meat or fish.

Serves 2

olive oil
2 garlic cloves, finely chopped, plus 1 cut garlic clove for rubbing
1 tablespoon dried oregano
a generous splash (around 1 tablespoon) Moscatel vinegar
750g frozen peas (garden or petit pois)
100ml chicken or vegetable stock (see pages 244–245), or water
2 slices of bread
salt and pepper

Heat a glug of olive oil in a saucepan. Add the garlic and oregano and fry until golden then deglaze with a splash of vinegar.

Add the frozen peas, stock and some salt and pepper, and cover the pan with greaseproof paper. Cook on a low to medium heat for 45 minutes, stirring from time to time, until the peas are soft, then add a glug of olive oil and adjust the seasoning if necessary.

Toast the bread then rub with the cut garlic, drizzle with a lick of olive oil and spoon the pea mixture on top.

Quail, sweet onion, cherry and almond on chopped chicken liver bruschetta

Robust and hearty, but elegant, too. You can get ahead with this by making the onions up to five days in advance and the chicken liver up to three days in advance (store in the fridge). If you want this to be lighter, serve half a quail each; for a proper lunch, have one each (the quantities of everything else will remain the same).

Serves 4

olive oil
4 quails (ask your butcher to spatchcock them for you)
20 cherries, destoned
4 tablespoons blanched almonds, lightly toasted and roughly chopped
100ml chicken stock (see page 245)
2 tablespoons chopped tarragon
4 slices of bread
salt and pepper

For the sweet onions
150ml olive oil
2 onions, thinly sliced

For the chicken livers
olive oil, enough to cover your pan when cooking both the shallots
    and livers
2 shallots, finely chopped
3 sage leaves
8 chicken livers
50ml Marsala
50ml chicken stock (see page 245)
30g unsalted butter
salt and pepper

First make the sweet onions. Heat the olive oil in a pan on a medium to low heat and cook the sliced onions for 30–45 minutes, stirring occasionally, until dark brown and sweet. Add a touch of water if necessary to prevent the onion from catching.

To cook the chicken livers, heat some olive oil in a pan on a low to medium heat and sweat the shallots and sage for 25 minutes until soft and golden.

Meanwhile, heat a frying pan on a high heat, add a touch of olive oil and drop in the chicken livers. Fry on a high heat on one side for 1½ minutes, then turn over and fry for 1 minute. Add the Marsala, 50ml chicken stock and butter. Cook for a further 60 seconds and transfer immediately into a bowl (if you leave them in the pan they will continue to cook). Roughly chop, add the shallots and sage and season with salt and pepper.

When you are ready to eat, heat a frying pan on a medium heat with a touch of olive oil. Season the quail with salt and add to the pan skin-side down. Cook until the skin starts to turn golden. Turn over, add the cherries and fry for 2 minutes. Add the sweet onions, almonds, some pepper and 100ml of chicken stock. Turn the heat down to low and cook for 25 minutes. Add the tarragon and check the seasoning.

Toast the bread, spread with the chopped chicken liver and spoon the quail and cherry goodness on top.

Fritti

Aaah, fried stuff: crispy and crunchy, sometimes gooey, and always golden. The naughtiest of foods and bad for cholesterol... but great for the soul. Indulge sporadically and you'll be fine. Considerations for frying:

1. Use neutral-flavoured and clean oil, such as sunflower, rapeseed or vegetable oil.
2. A deep-fat fryer is safer but if you're using a saucepan, make sure it's big enough that the oil doesn't spill over when you add whatever you're frying. Aim for a pan at least three times bigger than the amount of oil you are using.
3. If using a saucepan, a metal spaghetti basket is very useful as a fry basket.
4. Always take the pan off the heat when you've finished frying.
5. Keep children and pets away when frying.
6. Basically, be bloody careful!
7. No matter how many portions you're doing, always pane* in small batches and refresh your pane ingredients. This will ensure no clumps are formed and will give you that perfect, even crisp.
8. Have a suitable bowl or similar receptacle lined with paper towels ready before you start.
9. Always season any unseasoned bits of your pane – flour, semolina, whisked egg, etc – with salt and pepper.
10. A fried thing doesn't stay crispy for long, so eat quickly!

*Pane is one of those universal French kitchen terms used by all chefs. Basically it's the encasing of your fried ingredient, e.g. flour, whisked egg, breadcrumbs.

Mussel fritti

Popcorn of the sea: a moreish little snack that is very easy to eat and good for sharing.

Serves 4

about 50 mussels, cleaned (or ask your fishmonger to clean them
    for you)
a glug of olive oil
125ml white wine
300g plain flour, sifted
300g semolina
1.2 litres groundnut oil
16 flat-leaf parsley leaves
lemon wedges, for serving
fine sea salt

To clean the mussels, rinse them under cold water, scrape off any dirt, pull off the 'beards', and discard any mussels that are open once tapped or have broken shells.

Heat a pan big enough to hold all the mussels on a high heat and add some olive oil, followed quickly by the mussels and white wine. Give the pan a shake and put a lid on, and cook for 3–5 minutes until the mussels have opened. Transfer onto a tray (retain the cooking liquid) and allow to cool.

When cool, pick the mussels out of their shells, discarding any closed ones. Strain the cooking liquid through a fine sieve, then leave the mussels submerged in the liquid.

Get your pane ingredients ready: sifted plain flour, mussel cooking liquid and semolina. Fish out the mussels with a slotted spoon, then, working in batches, roll them in flour, dip back into the mussel juice then roll them in semolina.

Heat the groundnut oil to 180°C (or throw a breadcrumb in – when it sizzles and turns golden you're ready to go). Working in two batches, deep-fry the mussels for 2 minutes, then add the parsley for 10 seconds (stand back, it spits!). Transfer to a bowl lined with kitchen paper and season with fine sea salt.

Serve with a wedge of lemon for squeezing. Great with aioli (see page 241).

Rabbit with rosemary and orange salt

Finger-licking good for all the right reasons. This is a brilliant way to introduce kids to something aside from the famous four of pork, beef, chicken and lamb. You do need to find farmed rabbit – the cooking times for wild rabbit are different. Prepare the rosemary and orange salt at least two days ahead.

Serves 2

3 strips orange rind
2 sprigs of rosemary
1 farmed rabbit (jointed legs, shoulders, loin – off the saddle – and belly flaps; ask for a whole farmed rabbit, jointed)
500ml milk
500ml chicken stock (see page 245) or water
juice of ½ orange
6 sage leaves
2 shallots, chopped in half lengthways
10 peppercorns
300g plain flour, sifted
300g breadcrumbs (ideally panko but you can use any kind)
1.2 litres groundnut oil
lemon wedges and aioli (see page 241), to serve
fine sea salt

Put the orange rind and rosemary on a tray for 2 days until dry. (If you don't have time, you can dry them in an oven preheated to 110°C/gas mark ¼ for a few hours – check every so often to make sure they don't brown.) Whizz in a coffee grinder, finely chop or pound with a pestle and mortar until dust-like. Mix into some fine sea salt.

In a large pan, put the rabbit pieces (except the loin), milk, chicken stock or water, orange juice, sage, shallots, peppercorns and some salt. Place parchment paper on top, bring to a simmer and simmer for 45 minutes.

Remove the shoulders and flaps (the meat should be just falling off the bone). Cook the legs for a further 20 minutes (again until just falling off the bone). Basically, treat it like chicken legs, thighs, wings or drumsticks.

Strain the milky stock and allow to cool.

Get your pane ingredients ready: sifted flour, milk stock, breadcrumbs.

Roll the cooked rabbit pieces and the raw loin in flour, dip into the stock then roll in breadcrumbs. Heat the oil to 180°C. Deep-fry the rabbit for 2–3 minutes then scoop out with a slotted spoon into a bowl lined with kitchen paper. Season with rosemary and orange salt and serve with lemon wedges and aioli (see page 241) – and maybe some French fries?

Pig ear with anchovy

Don't be freaked out: once cooked down, pigs' ears become soft and unctuous and are one of the most subtle, delicious cuts of pork you will try; also, your butcher will love you because they always have too many! Perfect with a frosty lager.

The key to this dish is to use a large pot and to keep the ears covered with water at all times – it takes a while to cook but there's hardly any work involved.

Serves 4

2 pigs' ears, swabbed and cleaned
1 carrot
1 onion
10 peppercorns
4 bay leaves
300g rice flour
1.2 litres groundnut oil
anchovy paste (see page 240)
fine sea salt

In a large pan, completely submerge the pig ears in water, bring to the boil then turn down to a simmer. Foam will come to the surface: scoop it off and discard then pour the water away. Repeat this process a couple of times.

The third time, bring the water to the boil then reduce to a simmer. Add the carrot, onion, peppercorns, bay leaves and a pinch of salt. The ears will float, so place a hardy plate just a little smaller than the size of the pan or something else on top of them to weigh them down and keep them submerged. Simmer for 4–5 hours until totally soft. Check the thickest area of cartilage: it should have no resistance whatsoever when cut into – like a hot knife through butter.

Remove the pig ears from the cooking liquid and allow them to cool, then discard any jelly that has formed (this will spit in the fryer). Cut out the thickest piece of cartilage, discard, and then slice the ears widthways (across) into slices about ½cm thick.

Heat the oil to 180°C. Pane the ear slices in rice flour and deep-fry for 2–3 minutes. Scoop out with a slotted spoon into a bowl lined with kitchen paper and season with salt.

Serve with the anchovy paste as a dip (see page 240).

Shallot with gorgonzola fonduta

A fritti inspired by my favourite flavour of crisp, the mighty cheese and onion.

Serves 4

10 shallots, peeled and roots trimmed
4 sprigs of rosemary
300ml plain flour, sifted
250ml milk
300g semolina
1.2 litres groundnut oil
3 tablespoons gorgonzola
1 tablespoon crème fraîche
fine sea salt

Put the shallots, rosemary and a pinch of salt in a pan and cover with water. Bring to the boil, reduce the heat to a simmer and cook for 45 minutes–1 hour (until you can pierce the shallots with a knife with no resistance but without them falling apart).

Allow to cool and slice into quarters.

Get your pane ingredients ready: flour, milk and semolina. Roll the shallot quarters in flour, dip into the milk, then roll in semolina.

Heat the oil to 180°C. Meanwhile, heat the gorgonzola dolce and crème fraiche together in a saucepan on a low heat and stir until the gorgonzola has melted and all is combined in a creamy fonduta. Keep warm.

Deep-fry the shallots in a basket for 3–4 minutes until golden, then transfer into a bowl lined with kitchen paper to absorb excess oil. Season with fine sea salt.

Transfer the gorgonzola fonduta into a ramekin and serve alongside the deep-fried shallots.

Squash, chilli and taleggio

There are many varieties of squash that come into season in late summer and end around December. For me, the best are smack bang in the middle of autumn. Aim for deep orange-fleshed squash such as butternut or ideally Crown Prince.

Serves 2

¼ Crown Prince squash (400g), peeled
½ large red chilli, cut in half lengthways and deseeded
40g taleggio cheese, rind removed, cut into 2cm cubes
125ml milk
150g rice flour
1.2 litres groundnut oil
fine sea salt

Remove any seeds from your portion of squash. Use a mandolin or your sharpest knife to slice the squash into pieces about 3mm thick and 5cm long.

Slice the chilli into strips ½cm wide.

Keeping them separate, pane the squash, chilli and taleggio cubes in milk and rice flour.

Heat the oil to 180°C. Use a basket and drop the chilli in the oil for 30 seconds, followed by the squash and taleggio. Fry for 2 minutes, then transfer to a bowl lined with kitchen paper and season with fine sea salt.

Soups

I'm pretty sure every country in the world has its own version of a soup – whether it's borscht or bún bò huê, goulash or gumbo, miso or minestrone. What other category of food gets that global recognition? None, is the answer!

Anyway, here are some of my favourites. As ever, please for the love of God, where olive oil is called for, use the best you can get your hands on: it's a seasoning and is essential. Average (or bad) olive oil is a different product altogether and should never be used.

Fontina cheese, sweet onion, sourdough, golden garlic and Marsala

Inspired by Alpine fondue and French onion soup, this also goes down well after some form of outdoor winter activity (or if you are feeling the need to be gluttonous).

This soup requires some preparation so that you're ready to rock for last-minute assembly.

Serves 4

2 onions, finely sliced
a glug of olive oil
a glug of sunflower oil
3 garlic cloves, finely chopped
400ml chicken stock (see page 245)
200ml single cream
75ml Marsala
4 handfuls sourdough torn into bite-sized pieces
200g fontina, grated or cut into small cubes
salt and pepper

Cut the onions in half lengthways, peel and finely slice across into half-moons. Heat a large glug of olive oil in a pan over a low heat, add the onions and very gently stew for 45 minutes. From time to time, add water and scrape the bottom of the pan with a wooden spoon to prevent the onions from burning. You want onions that are dark brown, sweet and sticky.

To make the golden garlic, put some sunflower oil and the garlic in a small frying pan. Heat on a low to medium heat and continuously stir until the garlic begins to change colour – this will happen rapidly and you need to act quickly. When it's pale yellow, strain the garlic through a fine sieve placed over a bowl, shake off any excess oil and immediately spread out on kitchen paper to cool the garlic down. The residual heat will continue cooking the garlic and it will turn golden and sweet but shouldn't be bitter.

In a saucepan, heat the chicken stock, cream, sweet onions and Marsala for 5 minutes on a medium heat, then add the bread and fontina and turn the heat down to low – allow the fontina to melt before stirring. Add a good grind of pepper, the golden garlic and taste to check if it needs salt. Serve in hot bowls.

Borlotti bean, pancetta, Treviso and new season olive oil

One year, around November time, I was on a sourcing trip with my good friend Luca who imports some of the best Italian wines into the UK, and we stopped for the night in Treviso, just north of Venice. We went to a trattoria that, to all intents and purposes, seemed to have been closed for some time, which was slightly off-putting. The uncomfortable feeling intensified once we sat in the empty dining room and discovered that there was Mussolini memorabilia scattered everywhere. Nonetheless, we were hungry, nowhere else was open, and something smelled good. It turned into one of those meals in Italy – the one where you least expect the food to be good but it turns out to be a humdinger. This was one of the stand-out courses. (If you don't have new season olive oil then good-quality oil will be fine.)

Pulses are key at Trullo – whether in baking, boiling or roasting. See the chapter on garnishes (page 167) for more ways to cook with them.

Serves 4

120g pancetta, cubed
2 tablespoons finely chopped rosemary
2 garlic cloves, peeled
1 mug dried borlotti beans, soaked in a bowl of water overnight
  with a pinch of bicarbonate of soda
new season olive oil
1 medium potato, peeled and cut into quarters
1½–2 Treviso, shredded
a splash of Cabernet Sauvignon vinegar
salt and pepper

In a pan large enough to hold the borlotti beans comfortably, fry the pancetta, rosemary and whole garlic for 10 minutes on a low heat until it colours.

Strain the borlotti beans from their soaking liquid and rinse. Tip them into the pancetta pan and add a glug of olive oil, the potato and a good grind of black pepper. Cover with water by 2½cm and bring to the boil, then turn down to a simmer. Cover with parchment paper and cook for about 60 minutes, until soft.

Take the garlic, potato and a third of the beans out and coarsely whizz or pound or mash them together. Add back in to the beans and season – it should be the consistency of porridge. Put the raw Treviso in individual bowls, ladle beans on top and finish with a good glug of new season olive oil and a splash of Cabernet Sauvignon vinegar.

Chilled almond and Charentais melon

This recipe is inspired by my time cooking at London's Moro, and by the Spanish classic ajo blanco. Perfect for hot summers. It is critical to use ripe melons — if you can't find any then ripe raspberries, cherries or blueberries work just as well.

Serves 4

600g blanched almonds
about 1 litre water
½ garlic clove, minced
2–3 tablespoons Cabernet Sauvignon vinegar
8 tablespoons Charentais melon, roughly chopped into pieces
    about 3cm-square
a drizzle of olive oil
salt

In a food processor, whizz the almonds into a smooth marzipan-like paste. (You can do this in two batches.) This may require stopping and scraping the edges. Transfer to a mixing bowl and whisk in the water — make sure there are no lumps. Add the garlic and vinegar, then season with salt and whisk again until the mixture is thick enough to coat the back of a spoon — run your finger through the mixture on the back of the spoon and the line should hold for a couple of seconds. Chill in a fridge until cold. (Put your soup bowls in the fridge to chill at the same time.)

When you are ready to serve, you might need to add a touch more water and whisk again. Serve in chilled bowls and scatter melon on top. Finish with a small drizzle of olive oil.

Fish and bean soup

This summery soup is a cross between acqua pazza and ribollita and, like them, it can be super versatile – there are no set rules.

You can use any combination of fish and fresh beans but the ones listed here are my favourites. If you're using a fresh (or indeed dried) pulse, be sure to cook it first. Coco blanc and risina are available from July to September. If you can't get hold of them, or if you want to make this when they're not in season, you could of course use tinned or jarred cannellini or chickpeas – just start from where the beans are removed from their cooking liquid.

Serves 4

300g fresh coco blanc, risina or cannellini beans, podded
olive oil
3 sage leaves
300g Datterini tomatoes
½ red chilli, deseeded and finely chopped
2 tablespoons finely sliced fennel herb stalks, plus tops, picked
8 basil leaves
2 garlic cloves, finely sliced
125ml white wine
100g sea bass, filleted, skinned and roughly chopped
150g scallops, roughly chopped
100g red mullet, filleted and roughly chopped
100g sardines, filleted and roughly chopped
150g cooked brown crab, picked
2 handfuls sourdough torn into small pieces
juice of ⅓ lemon
salt and pepper

Put the beans in a pan, cover with water by 2½ cm and bring to the boil. Reduce to a simmer and skim off any foam, then add a glug of olive oil and the sage. Cook for 30 minutes or until soft. Season with salt and pepper.

Meanwhile, bring a pan of water up to the boil, drop in the tomatoes and leave for 1½ minutes, then drain and peel. Squeeze the majority of the seeds out (wear an apron and preferably do this outside!).

In a pan large enough for all the ingredients, heat a glug of olive oil on a medium heat and add the chilli, fennel stalks, basil and garlic. Fry until the garlic starts to colour then add the tomatoes. Fry for 7 minutes, then add the wine and reduce for 2 minutes. Now turn the heat down to low and add the sea bass, scallops, red mullet and sardines and cook for 3 minutes.

Remove the beans from their cooking liquid with a slotted spoon and add to the fish pot along with the brown crab, basil leaves, bread and lemon juice. Cook on a low heat for 2 minutes, adding a splash of the bean liquid if necessary. Season to taste.

Serve in warm bowls and finish with a drop of olive oil and a sprinkling of fennel tops.

Tripe, pig trotter, nduja, chickpea and cime di rapa

Inspired by street vendors serving tripe in Florence and slow-cooked cime di rapa from Puglia, and with a kick from Calabrian nduja salume, this stew-like mongrel is lip-smackingly good and ideally suited to smaller portions.

Serves 4

400g dried chickpeas, soaked in a bowl of water for 48 hours with
    a sprinkle of bicarbonate of soda
2 pig trotters, thoroughly cleaned and slashed all over with a knife
1 carrot
1 celery stick, cut in half
½ onion, peeled and cut in half
3 bay leaves
2 sprigs of rosemary
150g cime di rapa broccoli
2 garlic cloves, finely chopped
olive oil
1 tablespoon nduja salume
400g treated honeycomb tripe, cut into 5cm square pieces
200ml chicken stock (see page 245), or water
salt and pepper

Strain the soaked chickpeas and rinse. Put them and the pig trotters in a large pot and cover with water. Bring to the boil, then reduce to a simmer and ladle off the froth that forms. Add the carrot, celery, onion and herbs. Cover with parchment paper and simmer for 90 minutes to 2 hours. Add more water throughout the cooking time to make sure everything is entirely covered.

Once the chickpeas are cooked, take out and discard everything but the chickpeas and their cooking liquid. Leave the chickpeas to cool.

At the same time, strip the cime di rapa leaves off the stalks and put to one side. Finely slice the stalks about 1cm thick. Fry the garlic in olive oil over a medium heat; when it starts to colour add the cime di rapa stalks and reduce the heat to medium-low. Cook for 30 minutes until soft.

While the stalks are cooking, boil some water in a pan, lightly season with salt and cook the cime di rapa leaves for 15 minutes, then strain. When cool, squeeze out the excess liquid and incorporate the leaves with the cooked stalks and garlic and cook for 5 minutes. Allow to cool, season with salt and pepper, then roughly chop.

You now need a pan large enough to fit the tripe, chickpeas, chicken stock and cooked cime di rapa. Put it on a medium to low heat, add the nduja and melt. Now add the tripe and cook for 3 minutes. Add the chickpeas, chicken stock and cime di rapa. Stir while heating through and check for seasoning – add more salt and pepper if necessary. Serve in warm bowls with crusty bread.

Chapter 2:
Primi

Pasta

Pasta is many people's number one comfort food, but it also provides a healthy source of carbohydrate to fuel our bodies. Not only do I love pasta but I also respect it: you have to respect something that was created hundreds of years ago, has spread around the world, and brings joy to millions of people on a daily basis. What's more, we can choose how much we want to spend on it. It makes sense that it's universally enjoyed – who doesn't like pasta?

At Trullo, pasta is definitely the thing our customers love the most and it's integral to our identity as a restaurant. The flow of pasta production hums along as sure as the sun rises and sets. We roll around 25 metres of it a day, which is just under 9km a year. That's a lot of pasta and it requires hard-core teamwork, from combining batches of dough first thing in the morning, to rolling, shaping and filling pasta, chopping bases for ragus or making fresh ricotta – the list goes on and on. It's a full-on operation but our chefs enjoy making and cooking pasta more than any other job in the kitchen; I think it's because it ignites a sense of nostalgia within them and they can pass that feeling on.

When it comes to dried vs fresh pasta, it's not about which is better, it's about what acts as a more suitable vehicle for the component it's carrying. Above anything, it's about texture. Dry pasta has bite to it and is more robust, working as the backbone for the ingredients added to it, but it can also be less forgiving than fresh and will overcook quickly. Fresh pasta is more subtle and tends to either merge with its ingredients as one emulsified, delicious mass or wrap itself around a filling as a comfort blanket.

When I'm coming up with dishes for Trullo and it comes to pairing pasta shapes to sauces, I think about how the type of pasta carries the sauce and how it's going to feel in my mouth – for example, do I want a slurpy tagliarini with artichokes, or do I want something a little bit more robust? If I am keeping the artichokes chunky then I'd want a thicker ribbon pasta like tagliatelle, but if I'm whizzing them up into a purée, then I'd want to use tagliarini so it can combine together to be one mouthful (personally, I like the ease of just using a fork, which you can do with tagliarini).

On a trip to Tuscany, I was amazed by the different pici – thick noodles made with water, flour and olive oil instead of eggs – served everywhere. Everyone had the same ingredients going on in their dishes (parmesan and black pepper, olive oil or butter, or both) but each cook's pici had a different consistency and texture, and naturally everyone was convinced that theirs was the best. Some people rested their pici for ages, though one woman rolled it straight away. Whatever their method, they all said that it was exactly how it should be done. What this showed me is that there isn't a set rule for how to do things: everyone does it a different way. It's endearing.

In the south people tend to use more dried pasta, olive oil, seafood and shellfish, and the flavours are clean and light. The pasta in the north is more robust, with butter, cheese and meat – it's more luxurious (and expensive).

There will always be a place in my heart (and room at my table) for golden oldies like lasagne, carbonara or the mighty spag bol, but please consider exploring the potential of different pasta dishes – a lot of the recipes in this chapter have come from me playing around, so get creative.

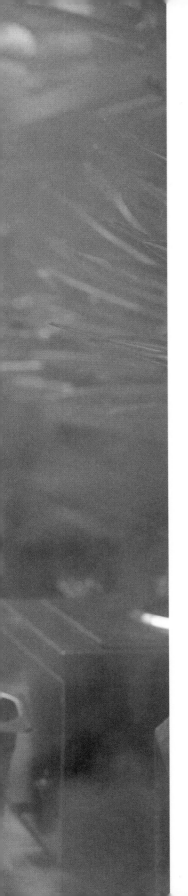

How to combine sauce with pasta

Before you start making your own pasta, or even just cooking really good pasta dishes, it's vital that you understand the proper way to combine your two main components – the pasta and the sauce. This method ensures that everything is well integrated and is tasting its best.

While the pasta is cooking, in a saucepan large enough to fit everything, combine the sauce ingredients (i.e butter, olive oil, ragu, broccoli, etc.) and add a splash of hot pasta cooking water and melt together – Italians call this 'la mantecatura'. Keep in mind this might take longer to warm up than your pasta to cook.

When the pasta is cooked, add to the sauce pan – making sure to keep the pasta cooking water. Vigorously toss the pasta in the pan for at least 30 seconds to work the gluten, adding more starchy cooking water as you go if it starts to dry up. By doing this, you create a silky emulsion with the aim of a viscous sauce that transmits the flavours evenly. Italians call this 'spadellare', literally 'sauce panning'.

Simple steps, but I promise it will transform the way you cook pasta forever.

Considerations for perfect pasta

Pasta water pan

One of the tricks to cooking excellent pasta (especially dried pasta) is to use a pan about five times bigger than the amount of pasta you're cooking. This allows the pasta to move freely and cook evenly. What's more, it's less likely to get stuck on the bottom and you can season the water correctly. If you are cooking pasta for around four people, invest in a pan about 30cm in diameter and 18cm high. This size pot will also come in really useful for cooking pulses and vegetables.

Pasta tossing pan

It needs a long handle and a heavy bottom, and for four people needs to be 25cm in diameter and 10cm deep.

Pasta baskets

Simple but effective, these round, perforated baskets with a handle sit inside a pan of boiling water and enable you to transfer pasta easily into your sauce, leaving you with the starchy water. No more last-minute panic to find a tea towel, or fighting for space to drain your pasta in a crowded sink: your toes can remain burn-free.

Dried pasta

We've all been there: the packet says ten minutes and you start checking after eight for the 'al dente' bite but it's raw. You check every 30 seconds until it's got to 11 minutes and it still feels undercooked. You leave it for 30 seconds more and then shazam!, your spaghetti is overcooked. You frantically try to mix it with the sauce but the al dente ship has sailed. How did this tragedy occur? Poor-quality dried pasta with a mixture of weak gluten flours is the answer.

Always check the label of your pasta: the ingredients should be durum wheat and water and nothing else. The pasta should be pale yellow – this indicates that the wheat is unbleached. I find the De Cecco brand is easily available, reasonably priced and does the job nicely.

Fresh pasta

I was extremely fortunate that I had Pete Begg and Jamie Oliver train me to produce fresh pasta – it's what sold me on wanting to be a chef.

It's not the most straightforward task, granted, but it really isn't difficult either, and it's so worth it for the end product. Making pasta has a communal vibe and is lots of fun for kids and adults alike – so get everyone involved!

If time is a constraint, spend 30 minutes one day making a couple of batches of pasta dough and divide them into meal-sized portions, then wrap thoroughly in cling film and freeze. When you know you want fresh pasta for a meal, defrost and roll. It's perfect for getting out in the morning before work or the school run, then rolling a later for supper.

Even better is spending some time rolling and shaping any of the pastas on page 94, portioning them into individual amounts, layering between parchment or greaseproof paper and freezing in a sealed container. This makes the ultimate ready meal – just add two to three minutes on to the cooking time. Alternatively, you can store them in the fridge, fresh, for 24–48 hours.

Seasoning pasta water

People are often unsure how much salt to add to their water. For adults, I normally say you want it to resemble mild sea water. I know this may seem like a lot of salt, but remember that only a fraction of the amount you add will be absorbed into the pasta. For children under five, I wouldn't add any salt to the water, and for kids over five, it's up to you to decide.

Add salt to water after it starts to boil – this way it will dissolve almost immediately so you can check straight away if the water is seasoned (if you add it when the water is cold, then you run the risk of adding too much).

Hot plates, mouths ready

You always want hot (or at least warm) plates to eat off and people sat down ready to eat. People wait because they think it's polite but you should start eating before it cools down and congeals – pasta waits for no man!

Adding cheese to pasta

There are a couple of recipes in this chapter that require parmesan to be folded into pasta instead of grated on top before serving. If you're not careful, you could end up with clumpy little balls of cheese – this happens when cheese is folded into pasta at a high heat and melts too quickly. Instead of folding cheese into pasta immediately, very finely grate it and leave it crested on top of the pasta (while still in the pan) and let the residual heat melt it, then fold it in, add a splash of pasta water, and you'll have a silky cheese sauce.

Portion size

I think pasta sometimes gets a bad rep because people serve huge portions, find themselves in a carb-coma, and get put off eating it regularly. How much you serve and eat is obviously down to personal choice but do consider your portion size. All the pasta doughs in this chapter are for a light meal and are always good with a simple salad.

Pici dough

Found all over Tuscany, this wonderful dense pasta is as frugal as it gets and really easy to make.

Serves 4

375g white bread flour
180ml water
1 tablespoon olive oil
pinch fine sea salt

Add the flour to a mixing bowl and make a well in the middle. Mix together the water, olive oil and salt and pour into the well. Start incorporating the flour into the water/olive oil/salt mixture until a dough starts to form. Once it forms, take the dough out, transfer to a clean table and start kneading it until it becomes smooth. With a rolling pin, shape it into a rectangle about 2cm thick, wrap in cling film and leave to rest for at least 30 minutes somewhere cool.

To make the pici, cut the dough into 15g strips (weigh one to check and use as a guide) and keep covered with a damp tea towel. On a dry, clean work surface – stainless steel or wood, you don't want something too smooth as a little bit of friction is important (a large wooden chopping board would do) – start rolling the strip outwards, with both palms of your hands, applying pressure evenly and pushing out, until you have a noodle the same thickness as a biro. Basically, you're making wriggly worms. Repeat until all the dough is used up. Cook straight away, or, if making in advance, store lengthways on a heavily floured tray (they stick together) covered with cling film and refrigerate for no more than 24 hours.

Plain pasta dough

This pasta dough covers the first couple of stages for all the plain flat and filled pasta recipes in this chapter.

Serves 4

200g 00 pasta flour
10 (140g) large free-range or organic egg yolks

Pour the flour into a mixing bowl and make a well in the middle. Pour the egg yolks into the well and, with a fork, start to incorporate the flour until crumbs are formed. Alternatively, put the flour in a food processor, turn it on, and pour the eggs in until crumbs form, then transfer to a mixing bowl.

Press the crumbs together with your hands to form a dough (if it's not forming, add a tiny splash of water). Transfer the dough to a clean surface and start to knead it with your hands for about 5 minutes until it becomes smooth and shiny. With a rolling pin, flatten it into a 1–2cm thick rectangle which is a similar width to your pasta machine, then wrap in cling film and rest it for at least 30 minutes in the fridge.

Pasta dough breaks up if rolled when chilled so allow time to bring it up to room temperature again and set up the pasta rolling machine.

If you're a beginner, you might want to roll the dough in batches of two or three. If so, cut your pasta dough into relevant sections and store them under a damp tea towel until you need it.

If the dough is too wet and sticks to the machine, dust it lightly with flour.

Stage 1

At the widest setting, roll the dough through the machine twice. Take the setting down by one and roll through twice more, then take the setting down once again and roll through a further two times. Fold the dough over, turn the setting back up to the widest setting and then follow this entire process two times over (this is to work the gluten to form a smoother dough and to achieve an even shape that makes it easier to roll).

Stage 2

Starting at the widest setting, roll the dough through twice on every setting until you reach the correct thickness for your shape, as listed on page 94.

Pasta shapes

Pappardelle – 1–2mm thickness

Sprinkle the table and pasta sheet with flour, cut into 20cm pieces and lay on top of each other. Turn, and then starting from the shorter end, roll up the layered pasta sheets into a tube. Cut into 2½ cm strips and shake through your fingers to prevent the pasta sticking.

Tagliatelle – 1–2mm thickness

Sprinkle the table and pasta sheet with flour, cut into 20cm pieces and lay on top of each other. Turn, and then starting from the shorter end, roll up the layered pasta sheets into a tube. Cut into 1¼cm strips and shake through your fingers to prevent the pasta sticking together.

Tagliarini – 1–2mm thickness

Sprinkle the table and pasta sheet with flour, cut into 20cm pieces and lay on top of each other. Turn, and then starting from the shorter end, roll up the layered pasta sheets into a tube. Cut into 2mm strips and shake through your fingers to prevent the pasta sticking together.

Ravioli – 0.5mm thickness or as thin as your machine will go.

If you're a beginner, you might want to do this in batches of two or three, so cut your pasta sheet into relevant sections and store under a damp tea towel until you need them.

To form ravioli, be sure to have a clean and dry table. Lay a pasta sheet out, and use two teaspoons: one to pick up your filling and the other to scrape the filling off the spoon onto the pasta sheet. The filling needs to be 1cm away from the edge of the pasta sheet and roughly 5cm apart from each other. Lightly brush the edge of the pasta sheet and the pasta between each filling with water, take the corner of the pasta sheet and fold over all the fillings by 1cm. Start at one end and form individual parcels around the filling, pushing any air out each time you seal – continue until all parcels are formed. Cut the edge lengthways where the parcels have been formed in a neat line and then cut the pasta between parcels to create raviolis. Cook straight away or store, covered with a tea towel and cling film, on a floured tray for up to 24 hours.

Cappellacci – 0.5mm thickness or as thin as your machine will go.

If you're a beginner, you might want to do this in batches of two or three, so cut your pasta sheet into relevant sections and store under a damp tea towel until you need them.

To form cappellacci, be sure to have a clean and dry table. Lay a pasta sheet out and cut 6cm squares of pasta, stacking them in piles of 3–4 at a time with a damp tea towel on top. Take four squares and lay them on the table, spoon-filling in the middle. Lightly brush two sides of the square with water and fold into a triangle. Seal the edges, pick up and hold the 2 bottom corners, push the centre (filling) in with your thumb, bring the corners in and pinch the corners to form a seal. Repeat until finished. Cook straight away or store, covered with a tea towel and cling film, on a floured tray for up to 24 hours.

Pici cacio e pepe

Cacio e pepe (cheese and pepper) is a classic dish from Rome and is one of our most popular dishes when it goes on the menu.

Romans use pecorino but we prefer high-quality, aged parmesan because it gives the dish more depth of flavour. But if you want to keep it traditional, swap the cheese in the ingredients list below.

Serves 4

1 batch of pici dough (see page 90)
160g unsalted butter
100g parmesan, finely grated
4 tablespoons freshly ground black pepper
1 teaspoon lemon juice

In a large saucepan, bring water up to the boil and season with salt to resemble mild sea water. Drop the pici in water and cook for 5–6 minutes. Meanwhile, add the butter, black pepper, lemon juice and a splash of pici water to a saucepan on a medium heat and then turn down to a low heat until they emulsify (melt into each other).

When the pici is cooked, remove it from the water and add to the saucepan with the butter and pepper. Keep the pasta water. Add the parmesan – but do not stir. Leave the parmesan to sit and melt from the residual heat of the pan – this prevents it from becoming chewy little cheesy balls. Once the parmesan has melted, stir the pici and sauce together to incorporate. Season with salt and serve immediately.

Pici with parmesan, black pepper and golden garlic

It's difficult not to eat pici when travelling around Tuscany – it's everywhere. For me, it is the ultimate peasant dish: just flour and water! But a handful of inexpensive ingredients transforms it into something really luxurious.

You need a few things at hand for this to be a success: you must have clean kitchen paper laid out on a plate (or something similar), a fine sieve, a large bowl and a steady eye for a couple of minutes.

Serves 4

1 batch pici dough (see page 90)
200ml sunflower oil
2 garlic cloves, finely chopped
80g unsalted butter, cubed
1 tablespoon ground black pepper
1 tablespoon chopped marjoram
25g parmesan, finely grated
salt

Prepare the pici dough and the pici, following the instructions on page 90. Bring a large pan of water up to the boil and season with salt to resemble mild seawater.

Put the sunflower oil and garlic in a small frying pan. Heat on a low to medium heat and stir continuously until the garlic starts to change colour – this will happen rapidly so you need to act quickly once it starts. As soon as the garlic turns pale yellow, strain it through a sieve placed over a bowl. You can reserve the oil for cooking with again. Shake off any excess oil and immediately spread the garlic out on kitchen paper to cool it down. Although the temperature drops quickly, the residual heat will continue cooking the garlic for a while and it will turn golden – but it shouldn't be bitter.

Drop the pici in the boiling water and cook for 5–6 minutes. Meanwhile, add the butter, black pepper, marjoram and a splash of pici water to a saucepan and place on a low heat until they emulsify (melt into each other).

Add the pici when ready, then the parmesan, but do not stir. Leave the parmesan to sit and melt from the residual heat of the pan – this prevents it from turning into chewy little cheesy balls. Once the parmesan has melted, stir the pici and sauce together to incorporate. Check the seasoning, then add the golden garlic, folding it in to the pasta. Serve immediately.

Farfalle with tinned sardines, cabbage, garlic and dried chilli

This was a staple when I was a student – as pasta recipes go, this one has got my back. It all comes together super quickly, so make sure you have your ingredients prepped and ready to go.

Serves 2

a glug of olive oil
1 garlic clove, finely chopped
½ teaspoon finely chopped deseeded dried chilli (or dried chilli flakes)
2 handfuls finely shredded white or hispi cabbage
juice of ¼ lemon
30g unsalted butter, cubed
2 tins sustainable high-quality sardines
4 parsley leaves, finely chopped
200g dried farfalle, or orechiette or penne
salt

To make the sauce, heat a glug of olive oil in a saucepan large enough to toss your pasta in later and fry the garlic and chilli on a medium heat until they start to colour. Add the shredded cabbage and sauté for around 4 minutes until turning soft. Add the lemon juice, take the pan off the heat and add the butter, sardines and parsley.

Put a large pan of water on to boil. Once the water is boiling, add salt to resemble mild sea water and add the farfalle. Add a splash of pasta cooking water to the pan of sardine sauce and put on a low heat until they melt together.

When the pasta is cooked, remove it from the water and add to the pan of sauce. Keep the pasta cooking water. Vigorously toss the pasta in the pan for at least 30 seconds to work the gluten, adding a splash more starchy cooking water if it starts to dry up. Continue tossing the pasta until the sauce emulsifies and has a viscous sauce. Serve immediately.

Orecchiette with purple sprouting broccoli, chilli and anchovy

Sprouting broccoli signifies the shift from the depths of winter, steering into the light. This is a warming dish for a cold night.

Serves 4

1kg purple sprouting broccoli
good-quality olive oil
4 garlic cloves, sliced
½ teaspoon finely chopped dried chilli (more if you want it)
1 tin good-quality anchovies
400g dried orecchiette or farfalle
salt and pepper
grated parmesan (optional)

Bring a large pan of water to the boil and add the broccoli. Cook for 7 minutes. Strain, allow to cool and finely chop.

Heat a pan on a low to medium heat and add a glug of olive oil. Add the garlic and chilli and fry until the garlic starts to colour. Add the anchovies and allow to melt for 3 minutes. Add the broccoli, put a lid on the pan and cook for 35 minutes on a medium to low heat, stirring from time to time and adding a splash of water if it starts to gets dry.

Remove the lid, increase the heat to medium and cook for a further 5 minutes. Season with salt and pepper and add a couple of glugs of olive oil.

Cook the pasta according to the packet instructions. Add to the broccoli sauce and stir, adding a splash of pasta water if the dish is dry. Finish with some grated parmesan if you fancy.

Tagliarini with dressed crab

This isn't a fluffy version of crab pasta – this crab has integrity and knows where it comes from.

Serves 4

1 batch plain pasta dough, for the tagliarini (see page 92) or 400g
   dried spaghetti or linguine
80g white cooked and picked crab meat
80g brown cooked and picked crab meat
1 chilli, deseeded and finely chopped
1 tablespoon finely chopped parsley
1 tablespoon olive oil
2 tablespoons lemon juice
50g unsalted butter
salt and pepper

Prepare your plain pasta dough (see page 92) and follow the instructions to make tagliarini (see page 94).

In a bowl, mix together the white and brown crab meats, chilli, parsley, olive oil and lemon juice. Season with salt and a good grind of pepper. Refrigerate until needed.

Bring a large pan of water to the boil and add salt to resemble mild sea water. Add the tagliarini and cook for 2 minutes (if using dried pasta cook until al dente).

Meanwhile, add a splash of pasta cooking water to a separate pan, add the butter and melt on a low heat, then add the crab mixture.

When the pasta is cooked, remove it from the water and add it to the crab. Keep the pasta cooking water. Vigorously toss the pasta in the pan for at least 30 seconds to work the gluten, adding a splash more starchy cooking water if it starts to dry up. Continue tossing the pasta until the sauce emulsifies. Adjust seasoning if necessary and serve immediately.

Tagliarini with baby artichokes

Early spring is the time for baby artichokes. They take less time to cook than larger artichokes because they are nowhere near as fibrous. The result is a light, fresh-tasting artichoke pasta with the added bonus that the baby chokes don't take as long to prepare!

Serves 4

1 batch plain pasta dough, for the tagliarini (see page 92) or 400g
  dried spaghetti or linguine
12 baby artichokes
60g unsalted butter, cubed
a glug of olive oil
2 garlic cloves, finely chopped
juice of ¼ lemon, plus a squeeze
20g parmesan, finely grated
10 parsley leaves, finely chopped
salt and pepper

Prepare your plain pasta dough (see page 92) and follow the instructions to make tagliarini (see page 94).

Peel the artichoke petals back until there are no longer any green bits. Cut in half lengthways – there shouldn't be much fluff inside but if there is, scoop it out with a teaspoon. Cut across into ½cm strips.

On a low to medium heat, warm a knob of butter and a glug of olive oil (this stops the butter from burning) in a pan large enough to toss your pasta. Add the garlic and fry until it starts to colour and then add the artichokes. Turn the heat up to medium, add the lemon juice and cook for 25 minutes, stirring from time to time, then season with salt and pepper. (If not using this straight away, you can store it in a sealed container in the fridge for up to two days.)

Bring water up to the boil in a large pan and add salt to resemble mild sea water. Add the tagliarini and cook for 2 minutes (if using dried pasta, cook until al dente).

Add a knob of butter, a squeeze of lemon juice and a splash of pasta cooking water to the pan of artichoke sauce and put on a low heat until they melt together.

When the pasta is cooked, remove from the water and add to the pan of sauce. Keep the pasta cooking water. Vigorously toss the pasta in the pan for at least 30 seconds to work the gluten, adding a splash more starchy cooking water if it starts to dry up. Add the grated parmesan to the top of the pasta, and leave for a minute to melt in the residual cooking heat. Add the parsley and continue tossing the pasta until the sauce emulsifies into a viscous sauce, adding more pasta water if too dry. Serve immediately.

Ravioli of sweet onion and squash with gorgonzola fonduta

As the days get shorter and autumn takes the reins, squash reach their zenith. This dish holds on to the last glimmer of late summer sun while providing enough comfort for the cold nights ahead. Serve with a glass of something that cuts through the richness, like a Chardonnay.

Serves 4

1 batch plain pasta dough, for the ravioli (see page 92)
2 onions, finely sliced
a glug of olive oil
¼ Crown Prince squash (400g), de-seeded
½ teaspoon finely chopped dried chilli
½ teaspoon ground cinnamon
1 teaspoon caster sugar
1 tablespoon marjoram leaves
3 tablespoons ricotta
2 tablespoons grated parmesan
½ nutmeg, finely grated
3 tablespoons gorgonzola dolce
1 tablespoon crème fraîche
8 parsley leaves, finely chopped
salt

Prepare your plain pasta dough (see page 92).

Cut the onions in half lengthways, peel and finely slice across into half-moons. Heat a large glug of olive oil in a pan over a low heat, add the onions and very gently stew for 45 minutes to 1 hour. From time to time, add water and scrape the bottom of the pan with a wooden spoon to prevent the onions from burning. You want onions that are dark brown, sweet and sticky.

Preheat your oven to 180°C/gas mark 4. Cut the squash into equal-sized wedges and lay them in a single layer on parchment paper in a heavy-bottomed roasting tray. Season with the dried chilli, ground cinnamon, sugar and marjoram and bake for 1 hour 15 minutes. You'll want to check from time to time and turn the squash – you want it to be quite dry with a dark golden crust. Scoop the flesh out of the skins while still hot, then mash with a fork and spread out on a tray. Leave to dry until cool (this stops the filling from becoming wet).

Season the ricotta with the grated parmesan and nutmeg, then mix the cooked onions, ricotta and squash together and check the seasoning. This will keep in a sealed container in the fridge overnight.

Follow the instructions to make ravioli (see page 95), using spoonfuls of the squash mix.

Bring a large pan of water up to the boil and season with salt to resemble mild sea water.

Over a low heat, heat the gorgonzola and crème fraîche together in a pan big enough to hold the ravioli, and mix together until the gorgonzola has melted and all has combined to create a creamy fonduta.

Put the ravioli in a spaghetti basket and drop into boiling water, then cook for 2 minutes and remove. (If you don't have a spaghetti basket just drop into the water and remove with a slotted spoon.) Add the ravioli to the fonduta along with the chopped parsley. Gently stir and add a splash of pasta water if it looks too thick (you want the consistency and movement of molten lava). Serve immediately.

Tagliarini with spicy tomato sauce

This is classic and simple, but man is it good — and always a crowd-pleaser. The key to success here is cooking the sauce low and slow — a little patience will transform what you thought you knew into something far superior. If you're after straight-up tomato sauce just omit the chilli. Be sure to use whole rather than chopped tomatoes.

Serves 4

1 batch plain pasta dough, for the tagliarini (see page 92) or 400g
  any dried pasta
500g tinned whole plum tomatoes
190ml olive oil, plus a glug
3 garlic cloves, finely chopped
1 red chilli, deseeded and finely chopped (more if you want)
½ teaspoon caster sugar
salt and pepper

Prepare your plain pasta dough (see page 92) and follow the instructions to make tagliarini (see page 94).

Strain the tinned tomatoes through a colander (the juice tends to be acidic and makes the sauce too wet — discard it).

Heat a glug of olive oil on a low to medium heat in a heavy-bottomed saucepan. Add the garlic and chilli and fry until just starting to change colour, then add the strained tomatoes and stir. After 5 minutes turn the heat down to low, add the 190ml of olive oil and the sugar and simmer for 2 hours. Stir and scrape the bottom of the pan occasionally to make sure the sauce doesn't catch. Taste and check for seasoning. You can store this sauce in a sealed container in the fridge for up to 5 days.

Bring water up to the boil in a large pan and add salt to resemble mild sea water. Add the tagliarini and cook for 2 minutes (if using dried pasta cook until al dente). Add a splash of pasta cooking water to the pan of tomato sauce and put on a low heat.

When the pasta is cooked, remove it from the water and add it to the pan of sauce. Keep the pasta cooking water. Vigorously toss the pasta in the pan for at least 30 seconds to work the gluten, adding a splash more starchy cooking water if it starts to dry up. Continue tossing the pasta until the sauce emulsifies to a viscous sauce. Serve immediately.

Gnudi of pumpkin and ricotta

We have this dish on the menu a lot in autumn. Light and nowhere near as filling as pasta, these fluffy little dumplings of happiness just melt in your mouth – you don't even have to chew!

Serves 4

500g deseeded pumpkin
¼ teaspoon finely chopped dried chilli
½ teaspoon ground cinnamon
½ teaspoon caster sugar
1 tablespoon chopped marjoram
200g ricotta
20g parmesan, finely grated, plus extra for topping
½ tablespoon plain flour
¼ nutmeg, finely grated
5 free-range or organic egg yolks, beaten
50g semolina
60g unsalted butter, cubed
8 sage leaves
salt

Preheat the oven to 180°C/gas mark 4. Cut the pumpkin into equal-sized wedges then put in a single layer in a heavy-bottomed, non-stick roasting tray. Season with the dried chilli, ground cinnamon, sugar and marjoram and bake for 1 hour 15 minutes. You'll want to check the pumpkin from time to time and turn it – you want it to be quite dry with a dark golden crust and soft enough to put a knife through with no resistance.

Scoop the pumpkin flesh out of the skins while still hot, then mash until smooth and spread out on a tray. Leave to dry until cool.

In a bowl, mix together the pumpkin, ricotta, parmesan, flour, nutmeg and egg yolks, then shape into little golf-ball-sized balls. Dust these – your gnudi – in semolina and leave in the fridge for at least 1 hour to firm up.

Bring some water up to the boil in a large pan and add salt, then drop the gnudi into the water and cook for 2 minutes. Gently remove the gnudi from the pan and reserve the cooking water.

In a separate saucepan over a medium heat, drop in the butter and a small ladle of the pasta cooking water and carefully add the gnudi. Gently stir until the butter and water emulsify into a silky sauce. Serve on hot plates and grate parmesan on the top.

Tagliatelle of smoked eel, lemon, cream and parsley

This recipe is dedicated to Fergus Henderson, as it was inspired by my time working at St. JOHN. Arbroath smokies (smoked haddock) were on the menu when I was there, and we baked them in double cream until the flavour infused. This pasta has a similar vibe but uses smoked eel (also introduced to me at St. JOHN), which is robust, meaty in texture and delicious.

You can buy smoked eel online, or from good fishmongers. I've used the Dutch Eel Company for years and find them to be the best. You can make the sauce up to two days ahead (store it in a tightly sealed container in the fridge), which will intensify the flavour, or serve it straight away – it will still be damn good.

Serves 4

1 batch plain pasta dough (see page 92), for the tagliatelle or 400g dried penne or conchiglie
100g smoked eel, filleted and cubed
250ml double cream
juice of ½ lemon
1 teaspoon ground black pepper
8 finely chopped parsley leaves
salt

Prepare the plain pasta dough (see page 92) and follow the instructions to make tagliatelle (see page 94).

In a saucepan large enough to toss your pasta in, place the eel, cream, lemon juice and pepper and warm on a low to medium heat. After 5 minutes, take off the heat and leave to cool down and infuse.

Bring water up to the boil in a large pan and add salt to resemble mild sea water. Add the tagliatelle and cook for 2 minutes (if using dried pasta cook until al dente).

Add a splash of pasta cooking water to the pan of cream and eel sauce and put on a low heat until they melt together.

When the pasta is cooked, remove it from the water and add it to the pan of eel. Keep the pasta cooking water. Vigorously toss the pasta in the pan for at least 30 seconds to work the gluten, adding a splash more starchy cooking water if it starts to dry up. Continue tossing the pasta until the sauce emulsifies and becomes viscous, then add the parsley. Serve immediately.

Squid ink tagliarini with steamed mussels, chilli and oregano

There's a little bit going on here but it is all straightforward enough. Give it a whirl: it's worth it and it looks totally cool.

You can also make this with a batch of plain pasta dough for fresh taglarini (see page 92). Or you can use 400g dried spaghetti or linguine.

Serves 4

For the squid ink pasta dough
20g squid ink
1 free-range or organic egg
1 teaspoon olive oil
½ tablespoon cold water
160g semolina
salt

For the sauce
olive oil
½ red chilli, deseeded
1 garlic clove, finely chopped
1 tablespoon dried oregano
32 mussels, cleaned and debearded (discard any open ones)
100ml white wine
30g unsalted butter

To make the pasta dough, put all the ingredients except the semolina in a jug and whisk together. Pour the semolina into a large mixing bowl and form a well. Add the wet ingredients to the well and start incorporating the semolina until a dough is formed and the bowl is clean. Transfer on to a work surface and knead for a minute or two until smooth. Wrap in cling film and leave to rest for at least 30 minutes, then follow the instructions to make tagliarini on page 94.

To make the sauce, pour a glug of olive oil into a pan, add the chilli, garlic and oregano and cook on a low heat for 30 minutes until soft.

Place a saucepan large enough to hold all the mussels (and for which you have a lid) on a medium heat. Add a glug of olive oil and, once hot, tip in the mussels. Shake, then add the wine. Cook uncovered for 1 minute, then put the lid on and cook for 3 minutes, or until all the mussels have opened. Discard any that won't open. Strain the mussels through a fine sieve over a bowl, retaining the cooking liquid.

Take the mussels out of their shells (discard these). Finely chop the mussels and transfer to a bowl, along with the chilli, garlic, oregano and reserved mussel liquid and stir. You can prepare this stage up to a day in advance.

Bring water up to the boil in a large pan and add salt to resemble mild sea water. Add the tagliarini and cook for 2 minutes (if using dried pasta cook until al dente).

In a separate pan (large enough to hold the pasta) heat the mussel mix and a knob of butter.

When the pasta is cooked, remove it from the water and add it to the pan of mussel sauce to toss. Keep the pasta cooking water. Vigorously toss the pasta in the pan for at least 30 seconds to work the gluten, adding a splash more starchy cooking water if it starts to dry up. Continue tossing the pasta until the sauce emulsifies and becomes viscous. Serve immediately.

Pappardelle with fennel
sausage ragu

This is a universal winner with meat lovers, and as easy as ragus come. Any leftover ragu is good on a slice of toast for a hearty lunch or for breakfast with a fried egg.

Serves 4

1 batch plain pasta dough (see page 92), for the pappardelle or 400g
    dried penne or spaghetti
1 tablespoon black peppercorns
½ teaspoon finely chopped deseeded dried chilli (or dried chilli flakes)
2 tablespoons fennel seeds
600g pork sausage meat
¼ teaspoon grated nutmeg
olive oil
175ml white wine
1 carrot, finely chopped
½ onion, finely chopped
1 celery stick, finely chopped
½ fennel bulb, finely chopped
4 garlic cloves, finely chopped
grated zest of ½ orange
bay leaves and sprigs of fresh thyme and rosemary, tied up
    in a bundle with string
300ml chicken stock (see page 245), plus extra if needed
2 tablespoons mascarpone
10 parsley leaves, finely chopped
parmesan, finely grated
salt and pepper

Prepare the plain pasta dough (see page 92) and follow the instructions to make pappardelle (see page 94).

Boil the peppercorns in a small pan of water for 30 minutes to soften them up, then drain.

Toast the chilli and fennel seeds in a dry frying pan over a medium heat for a couple of minutes, then tip on to a small plate immediately to stop the cooking process. Whizz to a fine powder in a coffee grinder (or grind with a pestle and mortar) then add to the sausage meat and season with the grated nutmeg and salt and pepper.

Heat a pan large enough to hold the sausage meat on a medium heat. Add a touch of olive oil and the sausage meat – you want a 2½cm-thick layer. You may need to do this in batches otherwise you'll end up stewing the sausage meat. Colour the meat until golden brown (don't try to rush this stage as this is where you'll create a lot of the flavour) then deglaze with a glug of the white wine and cook for a further 5 minutes. Transfer the meat to a container.

In the same pan, on a medium to low heat, add a glug of olive oil, the vegetables, garlic, orange zest, fresh herbs and whole boiled peppercorns. Sweat down until the vegetables are soft – around 20 minutes. Add the sausage meat back to the pan and mix together to make a ragu. Add the rest of the white wine and cook for 5 minutes, scraping all the goodness off the bottom of the pan. Add the chicken stock, cover with greaseproof paper and cook on a medium to low heat for 1 hour. Check every 20 minutes and stir, making sure to scrape the bottom of the pan to prevent it from catching – add more chicken stock if it's drying out. Once the ragu is cooked, check for seasoning and add the mascarpone.

Bring water up to the boil in a large pan and add salt to resemble mild sea water. Add the pappardelle and cook for 2 minutes (if using dried pasta, cook until al dente).

Add a splash of pasta cooking water to the pan of ragu and put on a low heat until they melt together.

When the pasta is cooked, remove it from the water and add it to the pan of ragu to toss. Keep the pasta cooking water. Vigorously toss the pasta in the pan for at least 30 seconds to work the gluten, adding a splash more starchy cooking water if it starts to dry up. Continue tossing the pasta until the sauce emulsifies and is viscous, then add the parsley and fold together. Top with parmesan and serve immediately.

Tagliatelle with rabbit ragu

The recipe below serves four but you might want to double it because it's also delicious on bruschetta or on a pile of buttery mashed potato and greens.

Serves 4

1 batch plain pasta dough (see page 92), for the tagliatelle or use
  400g penne
a glug of olive oil
2 large rabbit legs
½ onion, finely chopped
1 carrot, finely chopped
1 celery stick, finely chopped
2 garlic cloves, finely chopped
1 tablespoon black peppercorns
3 bay leaves
1 tablespoon finely chopped rosemary leaves
125ml white wine
250ml chicken stock (see page 245)
½ teaspoon grated lemon zest
½ teaspoon grated orange zest
2 tablespoons mascarpone
1½ tablespoons chopped flat-leaf parsley
grated parmesan
salt and black pepper

Prepare the plain pasta dough (see page 92) and follow the instructions to make tagliatelle (see page 94).

Boil the peppercorns in a small pan of water for 30 minutes to soften them, then drain.

In a saucepan big enough to hold the rabbit legs, heat a glug of olive oil on a medium to low heat, season the legs with salt and colour until totally golden. Transfer to some kitchen paper.

In the same pan, put the vegetables, garlic, boiled peppercorns and herbs, season with salt and a small grind of black pepper, and colour for 25 minutes. Meanwhile, preheat the oven to 170°C/gas mark 3.

Add the white wine to the pan, turn the heat up high, and reduce until you can't smell alcohol; add the chicken stock and bring up to the boil. Transfer into a casserole dish or heavy-bottomed roasting tray and add the rabbit legs. Cover with a lid or tightly with foil and pot-roast in the oven for 1 hour 30 minutes.

Allow the dish to cool and shred the meat off the bones into small pieces (be careful of the little bones). Transfer the meat back into the sauce, add the lemon and orange zest and the mascarpone, then check for seasoning and warm on a low heat.

Bring water up to the boil in a large pan and add salt to resemble mild sea water. Add the tagliatelle and cook for 2 minutes (if using dried pasta cook until al dente).

Add a splash of pasta cooking water to the pan of sauce and continue to warm on a low heat until they melt together.

When the pasta is cooked, remove it from the water and add it to the pan of ragu to toss. Keep the pasta cooking water. Vigorously toss the pasta in the pan for at least 30 seconds to work the gluten, adding a splash more starchy cooking water if it starts to dry up. Add the parsley and continue tossing the pasta until the sauce emulsifies and is viscous. Serve immediately, finishing with a sprinkling of grated parmesan.

Ravioli of calf's brain with sage butter

This is one of my all-time favourite pastas. I really like brains and how nothing else tastes like them. They have a unique flavour but, far from being overpowering, they are actually incredibly delicate and subtle. Gently cooking the brains and folding in the egg white gives them a mousse-like texture that feels good in the mouth.

Serves 4

1 batch plain pasta dough (see page 92), for the ravioli

For the court-bouillon stock
½ celery stick
½ onion
½ leek
1 tablespoon peppercorns
4 bay leaves
175ml white wine
juice of ½ lemon
1 litre water

For the brain
1 calf's brain
½ teaspoon grated nutmeg
40g grated parmesan
3 free-range or organic egg whites
40g unsalted butter, cubed
4 sage leaves
salt and pepper

To make the court-bouillon stock, put all the ingredients in a large saucepan. Bring to the boil, then reduce to a simmer and simmer for 20 minutes. Strain the liquid into a large bowl, discarding all the solid ingredients.

Gently clean the brain with a damp cloth, getting rid of any blood and/or bone. Poach the brain in simmering court-bouillon for 8 minutes. Gently remove the brain to a plate using a slotted spoon – it will be a bit wobbly – and leave to cool, then put in the fridge to firm up for around an hour.

Slice the brain in half lengthways and scoop it out of its membrane into a mixing bowl. Add the grated nutmeg, parmesan and some salt and a decent hit of pepper and stir together. In a separate bowl, whisk the egg whites to soft peaks and fold 2 heaped tablespoons into the brain mix.

Take your plain pasta dough (see page 92) and follow the instructions to make ravioli (see page 95), using spoonfuls of the brain mix.

Bring water up to the boil in a large pan and add salt to resemble mild sea water. Cook the ravioli for 2–3 minutes. Transfer to a large saucepan along with a splash of pasta water. Add the butter, sage and some pepper to the pan and cook until the sauce has reduced slightly and is silky and emulsified (you might need to add a splash of water). Serve on hot plates and finish with grated parmesan.

Tagliarini with raw green and yellow courgette, brown shrimp, chilli and lemon

Once the water is up to the boil this takes less than five minutes to pull together. To me, this dish signifies the height of summer and all its glory – good times.

Serves 4

1 batch plain pasta dough (see page 92), for the tagliarini or use 400g dried spaghetti or linguine
8 tablespoons coarsely grated raw green and yellow courgette
½ teaspoon fine sea salt
80g unsalted butter, cubed
juice of ¼ large lemon
¼ teaspoon finely chopped dried chilli
5 heaped tablespoons peeled, cooked brown shrimp
salt and pepper

Take your plain pasta dough (see page 92) and follow the instructions to make tagliarini (see page 94).

Place the grated courgette in a colander and add ½ teaspoon fine salt. Place a bowl under the colander and leave for 1 hour. Squeeze the courgette to extract as much liquid as possible.

Put a large pan of water on to boil. Once the water is boiling, add salt to resemble mild sea water. Add the tagliarini and cook for 2 minutes (if using dried pasta cook until al dente).

At the same time, in a saucepan big enough to hold the pasta, heat together the butter, a splash of the pasta cooking water, lemon juice and chilli over a low to medium heat. When the pasta is cooked, remove it from the water and add it to the pan of butter and lemon to toss. Keep the pasta cooking water.

Add the raw courgette and brown shrimp and vigorously toss the pasta in the pan for at least 30 seconds to work the gluten, adding a splash of starchy cooking water if it starts to dry up. Continue tossing the pasta until the sauce emulsifies and becomes viscous, and season with salt and pepper. Serve immediately.

Nettle tagliarini and egg yolk

Vibrant stingers start to shoot when winter finally comes to an end. It's time to pull on a pair of Marigolds and get trimming – what was once your childhood enemy will become a dear friend.

You want to use the young stingers you get in early spring for this recipe as the older summer ones are too fibrous.

Serves 4

For the nettle pasta dough
160g nettle leaves
1 free-range or organic egg
105g 00 flour
125g semolina flour

For the sauce
160g nettle leaves
60g unsalted butter, cubed
¼ teaspoon finely grated nutmeg
salt and pepper

To finish
90g grated parmesan
6 large free-range or organic egg yolks (stored in their half shells)

Pick and wash the nettles for both the pasta dough and the sauce, discarding the stalks. Blanch in boiling salted water for 25 minutes, stirring from time to time. Strain, then refresh in iced water and strain again. Squeeze all the liquid out – this is important. Whizz 40g of the cooked nettles into a paste and roughly chop the rest.

To make the pasta dough, whisk the nettle paste and whole egg together. Combine the 00 flour and semolina flour in a large mixing bowl and form a well. Put the wet ingredients in the well and start incorporating the flours until a dough is formed and the bowl is clean. Transfer on to a work surface and knead for 1–2 minutes until smooth. Wrap in cling film and leave to rest for at least 30 minutes.

Use the dough to make the tagliarini, following the instructions on page 94.

Bring water up to the boil in a large pan and add salt to resemble mild sea water. Add the tagliarini and cook for 2 minutes

In the meantime, make the sauce. Heat the butter in a saucepan large enough to toss the pasta in and add the remaining chopped nettles, a good grind of pepper and the nutmeg. Add a splash of pasta cooking water and put on a medium heat until they melt together.

When the pasta is cooked, remove it from the water and add it to the nettle pan. Keep the pasta cooking water. Vigorously toss the pasta in the pan for at least 30 seconds to work the gluten, adding a splash more starchy cooking water if it starts to dry up. Add the grated parmesan to the pasta, and leave for a minute to melt in the residual cooking heat. Continue tossing the pasta until the sauce emulsifies and becomes viscous.

Serve on hot plates. Make a small divot in the middle of the pasta and place a whole egg yolk on top of each serving.

Tagliatelle with sweetbreads, peas and mascarpone

Sweetbreads are weird little things, but they have a comforting aura to them, and peas add the necessary refreshing crunch.

Serves 4

1 batch fresh pasta dough (see page 92), for the tagliatelle or 400g
   dried tagliatelle
750g lamb sweetbreads
80g unsalted butter
a glug of olive oil
50ml Marsala
4 tablespoons podded fresh peas
3 tablespoons mascarpone
1 tablespoon finely sliced mint
salt and pepper

For the court-bouillon stock
1 celery stick
1 onion, quartered
1 leek, washed
1 tablespoon black peppercorns
3 bay leaves
125ml white wine
juice of ½ lemon
2 litres water

Take your plain pasta dough (see page 92) and follow the instructions to make tagliatelle on page 94.

To make the court-bouillon stock, put all the ingredients in a large saucepan. Bring to the boil, then reduce to a simmer and simmer for 20 minutes. Strain the liquid into a large bowl, discarding all the solid ingredients.

Pour the court-bouillon into a clean pan, bring back up to the boil and turn down to a simmer. Add the sweetbreads and poach for 3 minutes. Drain and peel the membrane off while they are still warm. Discard the stock.

Heat the butter and olive oil in a pan large enough to toss the pasta in on a medium heat and add the sweetbreads. Fry for 2 minutes, then turn over and cook for a further 2 minutes. Discard the oil (I do this by blotting the pan with kitchen paper), then add the Marsala and cook for 90 seconds. Add the peas, mascarpone, and mint, then season with salt and pepper.

Bring water up to the boil in a large pan and add salt to resemble mild sea water. Add the tagliatelle and cook for 2 minutes (if using dried pasta cook until al dente).

Add a splash of pasta cooking water to the pan of sweetbread sauce and return to a medium heat until they melt together.

When the pasta is cooked, remove it from the water and add it to the pan of sauce to toss. Keep the pasta cooking water. Vigorously toss the pasta in the pan for at least 30 seconds to work the gluten, adding a splash more starchy cooking water if it starts to dry up. Continue tossing the pasta until the sauce emulsifies and becomes viscous. Serve immediately.

Chapter 3:
Bbq

Bbq

My school summer holidays were as good as life gets: long, sunny days with my brothers and sisters playing cricket in the garden or on the beach relentlessly rolling in the surf. We'd never wear shoes or T-shirts and there was no worry of homework, school in the morning or even a set time for bed – just when to have ice cream. Most days ended outdoors, with the gentle plume of smoke from sausages, chops and wood as the sun set. A Bbq was my favourite type of meal then, and still is now.

My love of barbecuing was cemented during my time at Moro. Working in Sam and Sam Clark's kitchen was a real treat and I learned many things there, but one of the most important was how to use the charcoal grill and the possibilities and benefits of doing so. After that, there was no way I was opening Trullo without one, and the charcoal grill has become one of the main features of our menu. There really is no substitute for cooking on charcoal and wood – the smoky, charred flavour of meat and fish, vegetables, fruits and legumes is in a different league and, if you want to replicate Trullo cooking in your own home, I urge you to use a charcoal Bbq, drum or pit: it really makes a difference. We use predominantly charcoal as it is easier to store than wood, space-wise, and it distributes heat more evenly. That said, I understand the practicality and ease of a gas Bbq or a stove-top griddle, and the cooking methods in the recipes in this chapter also apply to these.

In this chapter I explain cooking techniques for different cuts of meat and fish, and if you look at the chart on pages 172–173, you can see what garnish they work with.

A Bbq can be way more enjoyable than what we're used to, which often consists of freaking out about cooking everything – burgers, sausages, chicken – all at the same time and then everything getting burned.

Often when people cook something like chicken legs on the Bbq, they start by putting them on raw and then they worry about whether the meat is cooked all the way through, or if it's burning on the outside while still pink in the middle. If you steam your chicken first or slow-roast a shoulder of lamb (you can do this up to a couple of days ahead), you just have to Bbq it for about five minutes and then it's ready. Doing it this way means you know it will be cooked through, but what's more, it will fall off the bone, it will be unctuous, and it will be tasty because you've put aromatics in with it. Even better, it's way less stressful: when it comes to your Bbq, you'll have everything ready to rock.

If you use your Bbq a lot you will tend to know instinctively when it's really hot. It's difficult to give exact timings, as the time it takes for your grill to be ready will depend on the size/surface space of your Bbq and whether you are using charcoal or wood. Here are some guidelines for a coal Bbq:

PEAK HEAT/HOT: the moment the flames die down but the charcoal is smouldering and bright reddish in colour.

MEDIUM TO HOT: 10 minutes after peak heat.

MEDIUM: 20 minutes after peak heat.

MEDIUM TO LOW: 25 minutes after peak heat.

LOW: 30 minutes after peak heat.

Tips

Tongs

I see people using spatulas, or those big outdoor tongs you get from the Bbq section of garden centres that don't have much give. They're hopeless! All you need is some small (around 25cm-long) stainless steel tongs (these will also be useful for removing pasta from its water).

Carving fork

We call this the 'fork of destiny' at the restaurant. With fish or anything delicate, if you use tongs to turn it, you tend to squeeze the fillet or the head, which breaks the fish up. If you use a fork to go in between the grills and underneath, then you can roll the fish over in one movement (or you can pick it up and then turn it over). This is very useful: I always ask new chefs to try it when they start and it really does make a difference.

Grill brush and clean Bbq

It's important to have a good, solid, clean grill brush because it is paramount that you always have a clean griddle (if not, things will stick to your grill or taint the flavour of what you're cooking). You need a decent brush: go to a garden centre or a hardware store to get the proper ones with metal bristles.

Using your Bbq all year

Although most people only use their Bbq over the summer months, it's nice to use it in winter too on a fine day. It's useful to have it to hand: keep it close to your kitchen door (if you have one), and use it as an extension to your kitchen. It's good as a heating cupboard: if you're making Sunday lunch, for example, you could grill a bit of meat on there or wilt vegetables. When your oven is full with other things, you can put your veg on there when the charcoal/heat has died down (or turn your gas Bbq off and put the veg in there with the hood down). Obviously at Trullo our Bbq is in the kitchen indoors but if you want to cook Trullo food, there's no reason you can't use your outdoor Bbq all year round.

Smoking/infusing (bowl and herb)

With any of the recipes in this chapter, if you want to add a bit of extra flavour, try a handful of hard herbs (rosemary, bay, thyme – whatever you want). If you have something like, say, a lamb rump cooking, put the herbs next to it, let them catch, then put a metal bowl over the meat and herbs. When you remove the bowl (do this safely), a big plume of smoke will come out. You need to do this towards the end of cooking, and only for a minute or two, but it gives the outside of meat or fish a slightly different smoky, herbaceous flavour.

Domestic oven back-up

Remember when you're cooking a lot of stuff on the Bbq, use your kitchen oven as a back-up for holding things and keeping them warm, or for finishing off the cooking – you don't need to squeeze everything onto your Bbq. That's when the flames start going mad!

Resting tray

Most of the recipes in this chapter talk about transferring whatever you've cooked to a tray. Whenever you put something through intense heat it is going to tense up, and the bigger the joint/piece of meat you're cooking, the more tense it is going to get. When you take your meat off the heat, it needs time to relax or it will be tough. The length of the resting period will depend on the size of your piece of meat, but I have given specific instructions for each recipe.

Smouldering

Once the coals have cooled to a lower temperature we often throw whole, unpeeled veg like onions, garlic, leeks, beetroot, or whole lettuce like radicchio or Little Gems, into the embers – they cook slightly and take on a smoky flavour. Of course you have to brush off the ash, or peel off a few layers before eating them. It's just a different way to cook using a charcoal grill.

Pork chop

Ask your butcher to cut the chops around 3cm thick and to take the rind off. Allow one pork chop per person; you ideally want to start marinating them 24–48 hours beforehand. At Trullo we serve our pork medium/ well done.

Serves 4

4 pork chops (rindless)
8 sage leaves
rind of 1 lemon
a glug of olive oil
1 garlic clove, crushed
2 tablespoons Moscatel vinegar
40g unsalted butter
100ml chicken stock (see page 245)
salt and pepper

In a bowl, mix together the pork chops, sage, strips of lemon rind, olive oil, garlic and a grind of pepper. Leave to marinate in the fridge for 24–48 hours.

Light your grill: the heat will be at its peak at the very moment that the flames die down – 25 minutes after this point is when you want to start cooking. If you are not using a coal Bbq, preheat your griddle to a medium to low temperature.

Season the chops with salt and grill for 12 minutes, turning every 3 minutes. Transfer to a warm metal tray and add the vinegar, butter and chicken stock. Leave to rest for 5 minutes somewhere warm, then transfer the chops to a plate. Reduce the juices in the tray for 2 minutes on either the grill or on a stove then pour over the chop. If you don't have access to high heat just pour the resting juices straight on the chops.

Calves' liver

We cook it medium at the restaurant.

Per person

150g calves' liver, sliced about 1cm thick and cut into 5cm pieces
1 teaspoon vegetable oil
1 tablespoon Cabernet Sauvignon vinegar
25g unsalted butter
50ml chicken stock (see page 245)
salt and pepper

Light your grill: the heat will be at its peak at the very moment that the flames die down – this point is when you want to start cooking. If you are not using a coal Bbq, preheat your griddle to hot.

Oil the liver with vegetable oil and season with salt. Grill for 2 minutes then turn and grill for 2 minutes more (or 3 minutes if you want it cooked medium well). Transfer to a warm metal tray, add the Cabernet Sauvignon vinegar, a grind of pepper, butter and the hot chicken stock. Leave to rest for 1 minute then transfer the liver to a plate. Reduce the juices in the tray for 2 minutes on either the grill or on a stove then pour over the liver. If you don't have access to high heat just pour the resting juices straight on the liver.

Pork ribs

A rack of 4–6 ribs is good for an adult portion. You ideally want to start marinating the ribs 48 hours beforehand.

Serves 6

1 tablespoon fennel seeds
1 teaspoon coriander seeds
½ teaspoon finely grated nutmeg
½ teaspoon finely chopped dried chilli
1 tablespoon muscovado sugar
1 tablespoon dried oregano
100ml freshly squeezed orange juice
½ garlic clove, minced
a good glug olive oil
6 pork rib racks (4–6 ribs per person)
500ml chicken stock (see page 245)
1 orange, sliced
1 lemon, sliced
salt and pepper, to season

In a dry frying pan on a medium heat, toast the fennel and coriander seeds, nutmeg and dried chilli for 2 minutes. Transfer into a coffee grinder or mortar and add the sugar, oregano and some salt and pepper, then whizz or pound with a pestle until dust-like. Mix together with the orange juice, the minced garlic and some olive oil and spread all over the ribs. Leave to marinate in the fridge for 24–48 hours.

Preheat the oven to 180°C/gas mark 4. In a roasting tray big enough to hold all the ribs, add the chicken stock and the orange and lemon slices, then place the ribs on top, cover tightly with foil and roast for 2 hours.

Both ribs and liquid need to be cooled and chilled, but separately: remove the ribs from the tray, let them cool and then refrigerate for up to 48 hours; leave the liquid to cool and scrape off the layer of fat that forms, then chill in the fridge and keep it for the gravy.

Light your grill: the heat will be at its peak at the very moment that the flames die down – 20 minutes after this point is when you want to start cooking. If you are not using a coal Bbq, preheat your griddle to a medium temperature.

Grill the ribs for about 5–7 minutes or until charred and crispy, turning constantly to prevent burning. Heat the gravy then serve in a gravy boat and tuck in.

Steamed and grilled rabbit leg

If you're hungry, I would allow for two legs per person, especially if the rabbits are wild as they're quite lean.

Serves 4–6

5 sprigs of rosemary
6 garlic cloves, crushed
200ml chicken stock (see page 245)
1 orange, sliced
8 rabbit legs (farmed or wild)
salt and pepper

Preheat the oven to 180°C/gas mark 4.

Put all the ingredients except the rabbit in a roasting tray big enough to hold the rabbit legs. Put a rack on top, sit the rabbit legs on the rack, then season with salt and pepper, cover tightly with foil and steam-roast for 1 hour.

Cool and chill the rabbit legs separately from the liquid (you can store them for up to 2 days in the fridge). Leave the liquid to cool and scrape off the layer of fat that forms, then chill and keep it for the gravy.

Light your grill: the heat will be at its peak at the very moment that the flames die down – 20 minutes after this point is when you want to start cooking. If you are not using a coal Bbq, preheat your griddle to a medium temperature.

Grill the rabbit legs for 3 minutes or until crisp and golden, then turn over and grill for a further 3 minutes. Heat the gravy in a small saucepan on the grill or on a stove and serve in a gravy boat.

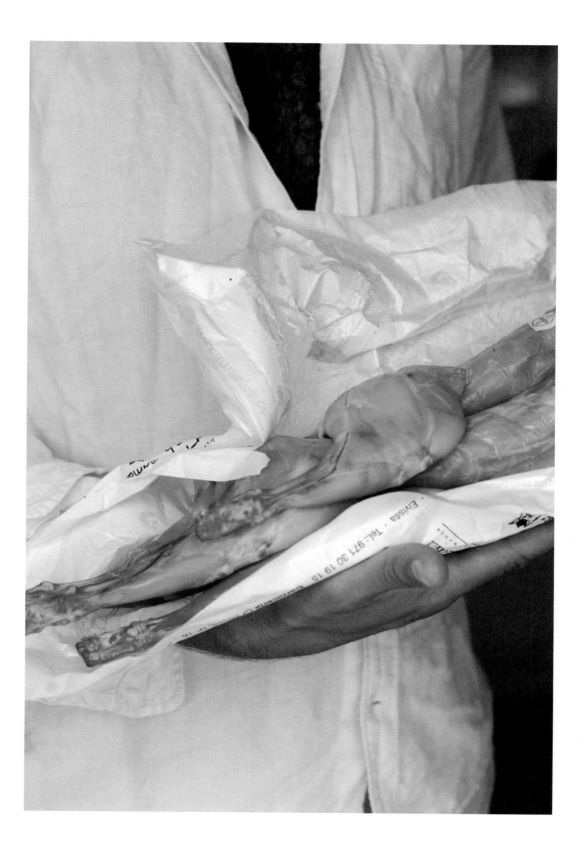

Steamed and grilled chicken leg

Depending on their size, I rarely find one leg enough when I'm hungry – two is better.

At Trullo, we steam the legs first in a load of aromatics for flavour and so the chicken is beautifully cooked and falling off the bone. It's then finished on the Bbq for 5–7 minutes to crisp up and get smoky – you'll never worry about raw chicken and burnt skin ever again!

Serves 4

6 garlic cloves, crushed
8 sprigs of tarragon
1 lemon, sliced
8 stalks of parsley, leaves picked and stalks retained
1 teaspoon fennel seeds
50ml chicken stock (see page 245)
20g unsalted butter
8 chicken legs
salt and pepper

Preheat the oven to 180°C/gas mark 4.

Put all the ingredients except the chicken in a roasting tray big enough to hold the chicken legs. Put a rack on top, lay the chicken legs on the rack, season with salt and pepper (grind twice as much pepper as you usually would), cover tightly with foil and steam-roast for 1 hour.

Cool and chill the chicken legs separately from the liquid (you can store them for up to 2 days in the fridge). Cool the liquid and scrape off the layer of fat that forms, then chill – keep the liquid for the gravy, discarding the herbs.

Light your grill: the heat will be at its peak at the very moment that the flames die down – 20 minutes after this point is when you want to start cooking. If you are not using a coal Bbq, preheat your griddle to a medium temperature.

Grill the chicken skin-side down for 3 minutes or until crisp and golden, then turn over and grill for 3 minutes more. Heat the gravy and serve in a gravy boat.

Lamb rump

Ask your butcher to slice steaks about 2.5cm thick. We serve our lamb pink. It's best to marinate the meat for 24–48 hours beforehand.

Serves 4

4 x 220g rumps of lamb, sliced into steaks
4 whole garlic cloves, smashed
4 sprigs of rosemary
½ teaspoon sweet paprika
3 tablespoons olive oil
1 tablespoon Cabernet Sauvignon vinegar
20g unsalted butter
50ml chicken stock (see page 245)
salt and pepper

Put the lamb in a large bowl, add the garlic, rosemary, sweet paprika and olive oil and mix together. Leave to marinate in the fridge for 24–48 hours.

Light your grill: the heat will be at its peak at the very moment that the flames die down – 20 minutes after this point is when you want to start cooking. If you are not using a coal Bbq, preheat your griddle to a medium temperature.

Season the lamb with salt and pepper. Grill for 10 minutes, turning every 2–3 minutes, then remove from the grill to a warm tray. Add the vinegar, butter and chicken stock and leave to rest for 5 minutes then transfer the lamb to a plate. Reduce the juices in the tray for 2 minutes on either the grill or on a stove then pour over the lamb. If you don't have access to high heat just pour the resting juices straight on the lamb.

Whole lamb shoulder

A lamb shoulder around 2.2–2.5kg will serve about 6 people. The key here is to slow-roast it in the oven first, then chill and portion it up to go on to the Bbq to crisp up. You could roast the lamb up 48 hours beforehand,

Serves 6

olive oil
lamb shoulder on the bone (2.2–2.5kg), trimmed of excess fat
2 carrots
2 celery sticks
2 red onion, peeled and cut in half
6 garlic cloves, peeled
4 sprigs of rosemary
5 bay leaves
¼ bottle white wine
300ml chicken stock (see page 245)
salt and pepper

Preheat the oven to 170°C/gas mark 3.

In a pan or casserole dish large enough to hold the lamb shoulder easily, heat a small amount of olive oil on a low to medium heat. Season the lamb with salt and gently colour until completely golden: take your time to get this perfect because this is a key stage and the foundation to flavour. Put the lamb to one side then add the vegetables and herbs to the pan and colour for 10 minutes. Add the white wine, turn the heat to high and reduce for 5 minutes. Add the chicken stock and bring to the boil.

Take a roasting tray big enough to fit everything in it and transfer all the ingredients, starting with the vegetables and stock and resting the lamb shoulder on top. Season with salt and pepper. Seal tightly with foil (make sure there are no rips) and slow-roast for 4 hours until the lamb is falling off the bone. Cool and chill the lamb shoulder until firm, separately from the liquid. Strain the liquid, cool and chill; scrape off the fat and use the liquid for gravy.

Cut hunks of lamb off the bone into portions. Make sure each portion has some skin and discard excess fat.

Light your grill: the heat will be at its peak at the very moment that the flames die down – 25 minutes after this point is when you want to start cooking. If you are not using a coal Bbq, preheat your griddle to a medium to low temperature.

Grill the lamb portions skin-side down until crispy and golden, then turn over and grill for 3 minutes more. At the same time, heat the gravy; it might be intense in flavour, so you can add a touch of water to dilute it.

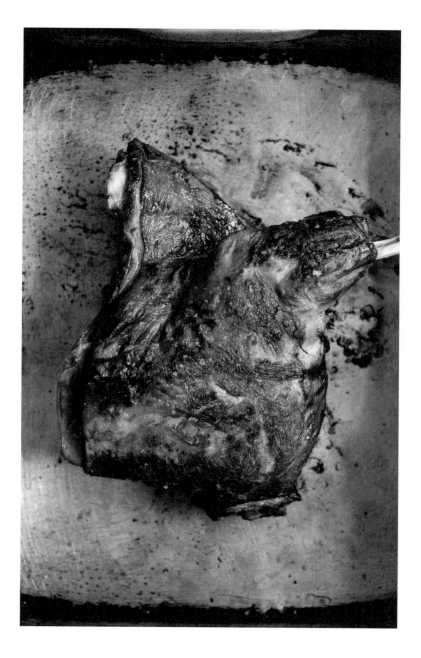

Veal chop

For me, this is a rare treat. It's totally possible to buy British veal: ask your butcher to source some or look on the internet. At Trullo, we serve our veal chops medium pink.

Serves 4

4 veal chops (approx. 350–380g each)
8 sage leaves
1 piece lemon rind
8 garlic cloves, crushed
1½ tablespoons ground black pepper
2 tablespoons olive oil, plus an extra glug
100ml chicken stock (see page 245)
4 tablespoons Moscatel vinegar
salt

Put the veal chops in a large bowl, add the sage leaves, lemon rind, garlic, pepper and olive oil and mix. Leave to marinate in the fridge for 24–48 hours.

Light your grill: the heat will be at its peak at the very moment that the flames die down – 25 minutes after this point is when you want to start cooking. If you are not using a coal Bbq, preheat your griddle to a medium to low temperature.

Season the veal with salt and grill for 14 minutes, turning every 2 minutes.

Transfer to a roasting tray, add a glug of olive oil, the chicken stock and Moscatel vinegar, and leave to rest somewhere warm or covered with foil for 8 minutes.

Beef onglet

Also known as hanger steak, this cut used to be called butchers' steak as butchers would keep it for themselves rather than sell it. It's a cut off the diaphragm and has become more trendy recently as people realise it's not all about fillet and rib-eye. Also, it's a fraction of the price (or at least today it is!). It is my favourite cut of beef to grill because of its deep unique flavour, a comforting mix of steak and background offal notes. With a high iron content and its lean attributes you don't feel nearly as heavy after eating – it reminds me I'm a carnivore.

At Trullo we serve our onglet rare. I would strongly advise you not to cook it any further than medium as it deteriorates massively – if you like steak cooked, don't use onglet. Ask your butcher to trim the onglet and portion it into individual portions of about 150g.

Serves 4

4 x onglet steaks, trimmed and portioned to 150g
8 sprigs of rosemary, slightly smashed
1 tablespoon freshly ground black pepper
a glug of olive oil
30g unsalted butter
4 tablespoons Cabernet Sauvignon vinegar
100ml chicken stock (see page 245)
salt

Put the onglet in a large bowl, add the rosemary, pepper and a glug of olive oil and mix. Leave to marinate in the fridge for 24–48 hours.

Light your grill: the heat will be at its peak at the very moment that the flames die down – this point is when you want to start cooking. If you are not using a coal Bbq, preheat your griddle to hot.

Season the onglet with salt and grill for 2–3 minutes, constantly rolling it over. The aim is to get it charred on the outside and deep purple on the inside. Transfer to a roasting tray and add the butter, vinegar and chicken stock; leave to rest for 2 minutes. Take the onglet out and reduce the liquid on a high heat for 90 seconds, then use as gravy. If you don't have access to high heat just pour the resting juices straight on the meat.

Mixed offal spiadina

You can choose whatever offal you like but you want everything to be roughly the same size so that it cooks evenly. Use the rosemary stalk as a skewer – this Italian tradition not only looks nice, but adds flavour too. You could also use wooden or metal skewers – if using wooden, be sure to soak them in water first so they don't catch on fire.

Per person

1 stalk rosemary
2 duck hearts, trimmed of sinew
2 rabbit kidneys, trimmed of sinew
1 chicken liver, trimmed of sinew
olive oil
salt and pepper

Hold the top 3–4 rosemary leaves at the tip of the rosemary stalk and pull away from you, taking the rest of the leaves off while leaving the stem intact. Cut the bottom of the stem on a 45-degree angle to create a sharp point. Leave the rosemary stalk to soak in warm water for 20 minutes to prevent it from burning on the grill.

Push the offal on to the rosemary stalk, alternating the pieces – for example, heart, kidney, liver, heart, kidney.

Light your grill: the heat will be at its peak at the very moment that the flames die down – this point is when you want to start cooking. If you are not using a coal Bbq, preheat your griddle to hot.

Lubricate the offal skewers with olive oil and season with salt and pepper. Grill for 3 minutes, turning continuously.

Wild sea trout/salmon

In the UK, sea trout season starts around May/June, followed by wild salmon over the rest of summer until September. Wild sea trout and salmon are beautiful and I would always recommend using seasonal fish if you can, but sustainably farmed salmon is at a respectable level these days. At Trullo we serve our sea trout and salmon medium rare.

Per person

160g salmon or sea trout fillet from the head-end (scaled, filleted and pin boned)
olive oil
salt

Light your grill: the heat will be at its peak at the very moment that the flames die down – 25 minutes after this point is when you want to start cooking. If you are not using a coal Bbq, preheat your griddle to a medium to low temperature.

Pat the salmon or sea trout skin dry, lubricate both sides with a thin layer of olive oil, and season with salt. Grill for 2–3 minutes; then use a carving fork to get under the fish through the griddles to lift and turn it, and cook for a further 2 minutes. Use the carving fork to take the fish off the grill.

Mackerel

I have a sweet relationship with mackerel. It reminds me of glorious summer holidays in Cornwall, dropping lines into the deep blue and having the thrill of feeling tugs and wriggles before pulling out majestic mackerel – two or three, sometimes even four at a time! Then sailing back to the harbour with salt-crusted eyelashes and sun-kissed brows, proud as could be and excited about the impending sunset Bbq. A day spent mackerel fishing is a good day.

I much prefer to cook mackerel whole because it gets a crispy skin while remaining succulent.

Per person

1 whole mackerel, about 250g
salt

Light your grill: the heat will be at its peak at the very moment that the flames die down – 25 minutes after this point is when you want to start cooking. If you are not using a coal Bbq, preheat your griddle to a medium to low temperature.

Season the whole mackerel with salt and grill for 8 minutes, rolling it over every 2 minutes with a carving fork.

bbq

Chapter 4:
Pan & oven

Pan & oven

My aim in this chapter is to teach you how to pan-fry a flawless piece of fish, how to roast a game bird to perfection and how to create sexy gravy out of the resting juices. I want to show you how easy it is to slow-cook a large joint of meat and have it fall off the bone so all you'll need to carve is a fork and spoon. Basically, I want you to become a Jedi in all things pan and oven.

Always use pans that are oven-safe, this allows you to get beautiful colour and flavour in the pan and then finish the cooking process in the oven. And it means less washing-up too.

Remember to use the chart on pages 172–173 and check what garnish works well with the protein you're cooking.

Partridge

When game season is in full flow, partridge is a mainstay on the Trullo menu. Similar to pigeon, partridge is widely available throughout game season. A little bit adventurous but not intimidating, it's a good one to try if you haven't cooked game before.

Whereas the legs on grouse are pretty spindly and lean without much meat, partridges tend to have chubby little legs; because of this, I find that when roasting whole partridge, if you want to cook the breasts perfectly then the legs will tend to be a little bit under-done or chewy, which is depressing. To work round this, at Trullo we usually take the legs off the crown and braise them, so that the meat slips off easily, and then cook the crown separately, throwing the legs in the oven at the end. This way you end up with crispy, unctuous legs that fall off the bone, and perfectly cooked breast meat.

Serves 2

olive oil
2 partridge, legs taken off and retained
¼ carrot, roughly chopped
¼ onion, roughly chopped
¼ celery, roughly chopped
2 bay leaves
½ glass red wine
100ml chicken stock (see page 245)
20g unsalted butter
1 teaspoon Cabernet Sauvignon vinegar
salt and pepper

Heat a pan big enough to fit the partridge legs on a medium heat and add a layer of olive oil. Season the legs with salt and pepper and colour in the pan until golden, then remove them and put to one side.

Add the chopped vegetables and bay leaves to the pan. Fry for 15 minutes on a medium to low heat. Add the wine and reduce for 2 minutes, return the legs to the pan then add the chicken stock and poach for 25 minutes on a low heat. Take the legs out of the liquid and set aside to cool. Strain the liquid, discard the vegetables and bay and keep the liquid for gravy.

Preheat the oven to 200°C/gas mark 6.

Heat an oven-safe pan big enough for the partridge crowns and legs on a medium to low heat and add a layer of olive oil. Season the crowns with salt and pepper, and colour in the pan on all sides until golden. Be sure to take your time to colour all sides because this is the foundation to flavour.

Add the partridge legs to the pan, then roast in the oven for 10 minutes. Take out and transfer to a warm tray to rest – the crowns should be upright with the fat end of the breast at the bottom (this allows the juices to flow back into the breast).

Heat the gravy, add the butter and vinegar and whisk together, reducing for 2 minutes. Pour the meat resting juices into the gravy and serve.

Grouse

Each season has its own charms, but the period when the leaves have started to change, summer is in its twilight and autumn is just beginning is arguably the best time of the year for produce. The 12th of August signifies the start of the game season in the UK and is fondly known as 'The Glorious Twelfth', and personally, the first grouse of the year is always a highlight in my calendar.

Of all birds, grouse has the most distinct, unique flavour. As long as you don't hang it for too long, it doesn't taste overly gamey, though you certainly know you're eating game. It's my favourite bird – you wouldn't want to eat it every day, but that's the point; it's a treat. You've got to get messy with it: get stuck in and use your hands. At Trullo, we serve grouse on the rarer side of medium.

Per person

1 oven-ready whole grouse (plucked, guts and head removed – ask your
   butcher to prep it for you)
2 cubes unsalted butter, plus extra for the gravy
2 sage leaves
olive oil
1 teaspoon Cabernet Sauvignon vinegar
50ml chicken stock (see page 245)
salt and pepper

Preheat the oven to 200°C/gas mark 6.

Fill the cavity of each bird with the butter and sage. Put an oven-safe frying pan large enough to hold all the grouse on a medium to low heat. Smother the grouse in olive oil, season with salt and pepper and start to colour in the pan. Be sure to take your time with this and to colour all sides of the bird, as this stage is the foundation to creating the most flavour.

When browned, roast in the oven for 12–14 minutes. Take out of the oven and put the birds into a warm tray to rest. The birds should be upright, with the fat end of the breast at the bottom (this allows the juices to flow back into the breast).

Deglaze the frying pan with vinegar, then add the chicken stock and some butter and reduce on a medium heat for 2 minutes; pour this over the birds and leave to rest for 5 minutes before serving.

Pheasant

Pheasant has a tendency to get a little dry and tough, but brining the bird for 24 hours (but no longer than this) works a treat by helping to keep the moistness in while also adding flavour.

Serves 2

4 litres water
600g salt, plus extra for seasoning
400g caster sugar
1 tablespoon bay leaves
1 tablespoon whole peppercorns
1 tablespoon fennel seeds
1 tablespoon mace blades
1 tablespoon cloves
1 oven-ready whole pheasant (plucked, guts and head removed – ask
   your butcher to prep it for you)
olive oil
1 tablespoon Moscatel vinegar
100ml chicken stock (see page 245)
pepper

Pour the water into a large pan and bring up to the boil, then add the salt, sugar, bay and spices. Boil for 10 minutes and then leave to cool. Submerge the whole pheasant in the brine liquid and leave for 24 hours in a fridge.

Preheat the oven to 200°C/gas mark 6.

Take the pheasant out of the brine and pat completely dry. Heat an oven-safe pan big enough to hold the pheasant on a medium heat. Smother the bird in olive oil, season with salt and pepper and brown in the pan. Be sure to take your time to colour all sides of the bird because this is the foundation to flavour.

Transfer to the oven and roast for 25–30 minutes.

Take out of the oven and transfer the bird to a warm tray to rest. Deglaze the pan with the vinegar, then add the chicken stock and reduce for 2 minutes on a medium heat. Pour the juice over the pheasant and rest for 10 minutes, covered with a foil blanket, before serving.

Whole lemon sole

A delicate and subtle version of its older brother Dover sole. I much prefer lemon sole cooked on the bone as it retains its sweet moisture. If you're lucky, there might be a little sack of roe, which is a Brucey bonus and should be celebrated.

One lemon sole serves one person, and ideally you need one large non-stick frying pan with a metal handle per fish. You can also roast the sole in a tray (this is advisable if you're cooking any more than two), but the benefit of frying the sole in a pan is that it gets the skin really golden and crispy.

Per person

1 whole lemon sole, about 250g, gutted and scaled
olive oil
juice of ¼ lemon
salt and pepper

Preheat the oven to 200°C/gas mark 6.

If frying in a pan, preheat one oven-safe frying pan per fish on a medium heat. Season the fish with salt and pepper, add a layer of oil to the pan and put in the lemon sole white-side down. Fry for 3 minutes then put in the preheated oven for 3 minutes. Take the pan out of the oven and turn over the fish, then add the lemon juice and leave off the heat to sit for 2 minutes. Serve sunny side up (white side) and spoon the juices over the fish.

If cooking entirely in the oven, line a roasting tray big enough to hold your fish in a single layer with parchment paper. Season the fish with salt and pepper and drizzle with olive oil. Lay the fish 'head to toe' (this creates more space) and roast in the preheated oven for 8 minutes. Take the tray out of the oven, then add the lemon juice and a drizzle of olive oil and leave off the heat to sit for 2 minutes. Serve with the juices spooned over.

Monkfish

It may be one of the scariest-looking fish in the sea but the true beauty of monkfish lies in its taste. It's so meaty that it has steak-like qualities and requires resting when it comes out of the oven.

Ask your fishmonger to cut you a piece from the fatter head-end, across the bone, and into portions: this section is more meaty and tasty. If you get a piece from the tail end, the cooking time won't be as long. You can comfortably roast four head-end portions of monkfish in a frying pan of 26–28cm diameter.

Per person

about 220g monkfish, skin removed and on the bone
olive oil
juice of ¼ lemon
salt and pepper

Preheat the oven to 200°C/gas mark 6.

Heat an oven-safe frying pan on a medium heat. Season the monkfish with salt and pepper, smother with olive oil and start colouring the fish in the pan for 2 minutes then turn and cook for a further 2 minutes. Put in the oven and roast for 12 minutes.

Remove the pan from the oven, add a glug of olive oil and the lemon juice and leave to rest off the heat for 3 minutes. Serve with the juices spooned over.

Turbot and brill

For me, turbot is the most extravagant fish in the sea. Not only is it meaty, gelatinous and robust, it's also sweet and has a delicate flavour – which is why it commands a high price. Brill is similar and also a beautiful thing: not quite as meaty and robust but still exceptionally good, and it tends to be cheaper. Either way, as long as they're the same size, the method below works for both types of fish.

Ask your fishmonger to cut tranche portions (where you have a bone in the middle and meat either side) of about 220g. You can fit four tranches in a frying pan of 26–28cm diameter.

Per person

olive oil
220g turbot or brill
1 sprig of rosemary, soaked in water for 2 minutes
1 anchovy fillet
juice of ¼ lemon
salt and pepper

Preheat the oven to 200°C/gas mark 6.

Heat a layer of olive oil on a medium heat in an oven-safe frying pan large enough to hold the tranches of turbot or brill.

Season the fish with salt and pepper and start to colour in the pan on the white side for 3 minutes. Put in the oven and roast for 3 minutes, then take out and turn the fish over. Add a rosemary sprig and an anchovy fillet to each tranche and return to the oven for 4–5 minutes.

Take out of the oven, drizzle with olive oil and add the lemon juice, then leave to rest off the heat for 2 minutes. Serve and spoon the juices over the fish.

Cod/pollack

In the UK we have a strong relationship with cod that goes back many generations, and feel very proud of this fine fish and its heritage (and rightly so). Unfortunately our love affair became greedy and supplies were massively depleted over the late 1980s and '90s. Stringent regulations were imposed on fishing in 2006, lots of influential chefs stopped putting cod on their menus and well-documented campaigns were introduced to educate the public about the negative impact of buying cod. The result has seen stock levels increase and today, as long as we regularly mix up the types of fish we buy and consume, it's safe for cod to be back on the menu.

Pollack is closely related to cod and though it doesn't have quite the same depth of flavour it is still a mighty fine fish, and more affordable.

Per person

130g cod or pollack fillet, scaled and pin-boned
olive oil
juice of ¼ lemon
salt and pepper

Heat a frying pan on a medium heat with a layer of olive oil. Pat the skin dry, smother with olive oil and season with salt and pepper.

Add the cod or pollack to the pan skin-side down and fry for 2 minutes, then turn the heat down to medium-low and continue to fry for a further 3 minutes. Turn over and fry for 3 minutes. Take the fish off the heat, add the lemon juice and allow to sit for 90 seconds. Serve and spoon the juices over the fish.

Pork shoulder

Pure indulgence and a serious crowd pleaser — you need a gang of people to get through this (eight is a good number) and that nearly always leads to fun times. This recipe is ideal for Sunday lunch because you can put it in the oven before you go to bed on Saturday and leave it to roast slow and low, self-basting while you sleep. Waking up to the aroma of crackled pig is one of the finest ways to start a day, in my opinion. Take it out of the oven around 10am, cover with foil and leave it to sit somewhere warm — it will retain its heat for a couple of hours and you're free to crack on with your roasties. It's also a great alternative to turkey or goose for Christmas Day lunch.

Serves 8

2 tablespoons fennel seeds
1 whole dried chilli, deseeded and finely chopped
2 teaspoons salt
whole pork shoulder on the bone, about 4kg (ask your butcher
    to score the skin 3cm apart)

Toast the fennel seeds and chilli in a dry frying pan over a medium heat for 2–3 minutes. Transfer to a mortar, add salt and coarsely pound with a pestle. Rub into the pork shoulder, making sure to get in between the scored lines. Leave to marinate in the fridge for at least 3 hours, and up to 24 hours.

Preheat the oven to 220°C/gas mark 7.

Put a rack inside a roasting tray big enough to comfortably hold the pork shoulder. Put the shoulder on the rack, pat dry with kitchen paper and roast for 30–45 minutes (for the skin to start to crackle). Turn the heat down all the way to 110°C/gas mark ¼ and leave to cook for 8–10 hours.

Whole lamb shoulder

This is so tasty and so easy to make – always a winner. It's perfect for groups of 4–6, and kids love it too.

Cooking for large numbers of people doesn't need to be an ordeal. One way to reduce the stress is to do as much as you can in advance. For example, if you're doing a roast for family or having friends round for Sunday lunch, you can cook your lamb shoulder on Friday or Saturday, when you're relaxed and have the time to do it. Literally cook everything in the roasting tray, then chill the whole thing in the tray in the fridge, and when people come round all you have to do is pop it in the oven for 30 minutes or until the lamb is falling off the bone. It's like a homemade ready-meal: no fuss, most of your washing-up is done beforehand, and you're free to have a good time.

Leftovers – if you have any – are perfect for lamb broth (throw in some pearl barley or farro to bulk it out).

Serves 4–6

olive oil
lamb shoulder on the bone, trimmed of any excess fat
10 garlic cloves, roughly chopped
2 carrots, roughly chopped
2 celery sticks, roughly chopped
6 Roseval or Desiree potatoes, roughly chopped
2 red onions, roughly chopped
4 sprigs of rosemary
5 bay leaves
¼ bottle of white wine
300ml chicken stock (see page 245)
salt and pepper

Preheat the oven to 170°C/gas mark 3.

In a pan large enough to easily take the lamb shoulder and vegetables, heat a small amount of olive oil on a low to medium heat. Season the lamb with salt and gently colour until completely golden. Take your time to get this perfect because this is a key stage and the foundation to flavour.

Take the lamb out of the pan and put to one side, add the vegetables and herbs to the pan and colour for 10 minutes. Add the white wine and turn the heat to high, then reduce for 5 minutes. Add the chicken stock and bring to the boil.

Transfer everything to a roasting tray big enough to fit the lamb and veg – start with the vegetables and stock and rest the lamb shoulder on top. Season with salt and pepper then seal tightly with foil (be sure there are no rips). Slow-roast for 3½ hours then remove the foil and increase the heat to 200°C/gas mark 6 and roast for 30 minutes more, basting from time to time.

Chapter 5:
Garnishes

Garnishes

In the kitchen at Trullo we have many multitasking garnishes. Castelluccio lentils and salsa rossa, for example (see page 174), is as delightful with grilled mackerel as it is served alongside slow-cooked lamb shoulder.

I reckoned the best way to communicate the range and adaptability of Trullo's garnishes (or what you might call side dishes) at home was to create the chart on pages 172–173. The aim is for you to have flexibility and to choose what you want to eat with what; you can also use the chart as a reference point for putting together flavour combinations that work well. Hopefully it will inspire you to get cooking, whether it's recipes from this book, other cookbooks, or your own creative inventions!

As always, it's a given that the higher the quality of the produce that you use, the better start you have when starting to cook. But you also need to consider the foundations. Soffritto is a term used for the base of many dishes – in essence, it's the foundation of your dish – and can be made up of any number of ingredients. Cooking a simple mixture of finely chopped carrot, onion and celery (the classic ingredients) slowly allows the vegetables' natural sugars to release. Scraping the sticky vegetal goodness (natural Oxo before it's cubed!) from the bottom of the pan will give you a far superior end product – patience and calm is required but it's certainly not difficult. Like many things in life, build on sound foundations and it won't let you down.

Following cooking techniques through and being disciplined is also crucial to creating layers of flavour. It's tempting to let impatience get the better of you, especially when you're in a rush, but taking your time to get an even golden colour on the Little Gem in the grilled Little Gem, peas, pancetta and mint (see page 179) will ensure you're extracting and sealing in all that flavour; similarly, allowing peppers to steam in a bowl sealed with cling film continues the cooking process while retaining all the flavour.

This chapter is designed to help you to put together a whole meal, but these recipes don't have to be sidelined to the position of supporting actor. All of these dishes stand up by themselves as a quick snack or a light lunch. For a more filling meal, you can put them on a bruschetta or fold them through pasta. Though they are delicious as they are, on the following page you will find some additional ideas for making some of these garnishes the main event.

Castelluccio lentils and salsa rossa (page 174): top with goat's curd or fold through watercress, beetroot, roast pumpkin or roast aubergine.

Braised fennel and purple olive dressing (page 176): roughly chop up and fold through spaghetti or tagliatelle, spoon over polenta or bake in the oven (top with parmesan cheese and cream once it is hot) to make a little gratin.

Grilled Little Gem, peas, pancetta and mint (page 179): add vegetable or chicken stock to turn it into a soup (a handful of beans thrown in there would help it).

Poached potato, grilled radicchio, oregano and anchovy (page 180): turn into soup or fold into whisked eggs and then bake to make a frittata.

Braised hispi cabbage, clams, chilli and oregano (page 182): chop up and put through a salad, or add some water or stock to turn it into a soup.

Cannellini beans, King cabbage and pancetta (page 184): lovely on a bruschetta, or turn into pasta e fagioli – once cooked, keep hot and drop in some rough ends of pasta until done.

Runner beans, red pepper, basil and crème fraîche (page 192): fold through cooked potatoes to make a potato salad.

Baked borlotti beans, coco blanc or cannellini and salsa rossa/ verde (page 195): add to salads, pasta, bruschetta, fish cakes, bean burgers, risotto...

	Pork	Beef/veal	Chicken/rabbit
Castelluccio lentils and salsa rossa	●	●	●
Braised fennel and purple olive dressing			
Tomato, cucumber, red pepper and bread salad			●
Grilled Little Gem, peas, pancetta and mint			
Poached potato, radicchio, oregano and anchovy	●	●	●
Braised hispi cabbage, clams, chilli and oregano			
Cannellini beans, King cabbage and pancetta	●		
Dijon mashed potato, grilled marinated radicchio and pickled red onion	●		●
Roseval potato, red pepper, anchovy, olive, chilli and rosemary al forno		●	●
Castelluccio lentils, chopped chicken liver and fig crostini			
Runner beans, grilled marinated red pepper, basil and crème fraîche	●	●	●
Stewed bobby beans	●	●	●
Baked borlotti beans and salsa rossa/verde	●	●	●

Game birds	Lamb	Offal	Oily fish (mackerel, salmon, trout)	Meaty fish (turbot, monkfish, brill, bass)	Flaky fish (lemon sole, red mullet, pollack)
●	●	●	●	●	●
	●		●	●	
			●		
	●				●
	●				
			●	●	●
●		●		●	●
		●			
	●				
●					
	●				
●	●	●			
●	●	●			

Castelluccio lentils and salsa rossa

This dish has been with us at Trullo from the beginning: our chefs call it 'el classico' and it often shows up on the menu.

Castelluccio is a town in Umbria, central Italy, and the area is famous for its lentils. These are more robust and hearty than most lentils, with a wonderful deep flavour and nuttiness to them, and they require a longer cooking time.

Serves 4

a couple of glugs of olive oil
½ onion, finely chopped
1 carrot, finely chopped
½ celery stick, finely chopped
2 garlic cloves, finely chopped
1 teaspoon smoked paprika
4 bay leaves
440g dried Castelluccio lentils
20ml Cabernet Sauvignon vinegar
10 leaves parsley, picked and finely chopped
salsa rossa (see page 239)

Heat a saucepan large enough to hold the lentils on a low heat and add a glug of olive oil, the vegetables, paprika and bay leaves. Sweat for 30 minutes, slow and low – the natural sugars will release and start to caramelise, creating a flavoursome foundation that makes all the difference to the end product. Your aim is to end with a soft, vegetal mass – if it looks as though it's starting to catch and take on too much colour, add a splash of water and take off the heat for a moment to allow the temperature to come down, and then you can start again (control the heat, don't let it control you!).

Stir in the lentils, then turn the heat up to medium and add about a tablespoon of vinegar. Stir for 30 seconds and add water to cover the lentils by 2½cm. Cover with parchment paper, turn the heat down low and simmer for 30–40 minutes. The lentils should have a tiny bite left in them.

Add the parsley, a glug of olive oil and about a teaspoon of vinegar, and season with salt and pepper.

To make the salsa rossa, see page 239. Serve the salsa as a lightning strike across the lentils.

Braised fennel and purple olive dressing

This braised fennel is comforting and unctuous while still managing to retain an element of freshness and zing.

Serves 4

6 fennel bulbs
a couple of glugs of olive oil
2 garlic cloves, finely chopped
1 tablespoon fennel seeds
juice of ½ lemon
salt and pepper
purple olive dressing (see page 240)

Pick the fennel tops off and put to one side. Remove the outer, fibrous fennel layer (you can save these for vegetable stock). Cut the bulbs into quarters.

Heat a pan large enough to hold the fennel on a low to medium heat, then add a glug of olive oil and the garlic and fennel seeds. Sweat for 2–3 minutes until the garlic starts to colour. Add the fennel quarters and lemon juice, season with salt and pepper and stir. Cover with parchment paper and cook for 40 minutes until soft – add a splash of water from time to time if it looks like it's drying out and catching at the bottom of the pan.

While the fennel cooks, make the purple olive dressing, see page 240. Once the fennel is ready, add a glug of olive oil and check the seasoning, adding a touch more lemon if you want more zing. Spoon the dressing over the plated fennel and garnish with the fennel tops.

Tomato, cucumber, red pepper and bread salad

This salad always makes me think of sunshine-filled days, shoes off and eating outdoors.

Serves 2

3 red peppers
olive oil
3 sunny ripe tomatoes
1 tablespoon Cabernet Sauvignon vinegar
15g (around 1 slice) good-quality stale bread, torn into small
    pieces around 1cm
½ cucumber
8 basil leaves
salt and pepper

Grill the whole peppers, or roast them in an oven preheated to 180°C/gas mark 4, until wrinkled or charred. Put them in a bowl and cover with cling film. Let the peppers cool down until you can handle them (not until cold) and rub the skins off and deseed. Roughly slice into strips.

Heat a pan over a low to medium heat and add a glug of olive oil and the grilled red peppers. Slowly cook for 25 minutes until soft and sticky (add a splash of water from time to time to prevent burning), then leave to cool.

Roughly chop the tomatoes into 4cm pieces, squeeze out the seeds and discard them. Put in a mixing bowl, add a glug of olive oil, a pinch of salt, a splash of vinegar and stir. Leave for 5 minutes for the salt to draw the juice from the tomatoes and create a natural dressing, then add the bread and stir.

Tiger-stripe the cucumber with a peeler, cut in half lengthways, scoop out and discard the seeds, then roughly chop into 2cm-thick pieces. Add to the mixing bowl, along with the red peppers and basil. Mix together: the bread is not meant to be crouton-like but to add texture to the dish, so be sure it's mushed up. Check for seasoning and add a touch of olive oil and vinegar if it needs it.

Grilled Little Gem, peas, pancetta and mint

This could pass for a light lunch or snack by itself on a bruschetta. For something more filling, roughly chop and toss through some pasta.

Serves 4

4 Little Gem lettuce, cut in half lengthways
olive oil
50g pancetta, cut into 2cm pieces
1 bunch mint, stalks and leaves separated and finely chopped
3 garlic cloves, finely chopped
100ml chicken or vegetable stock (see pages 244–245)
100g fresh peas, podded
1 tablespoon Moscatel vinegar
20g unsalted butter
salt

Heat a Bbq, griddle pan or frying pan to a medium heat.

Rub oil on the cut side of the Little Gem and season with salt. Put on the grill or pan and colour for 3 minutes, then turn over and continue cooking for 2 minutes before taking off the heat.

Heat a pan big enough to hold the Little Gem and the peas on a medium heat. Add the pancetta and mint stalks and fry for 2 minutes until starting to colour. Next add the garlic and fry for 2–3 minutes until just starting to turn golden, then add the stock and bring to the boil. Add the peas and Little Gem, season with salt and pepper and turn down to a gentle simmer – cover with parchment paper and cook for 10 minutes.

Stir in the vinegar, butter and chopped mint leaves and check for seasoning.

Poached potato, grilled radicchio, oregano and anchovy

As far as spuds go, this is quite a grown-up, lavish dish – and very moreish. A good one for dinner parties.

Serves 4

3 litres chicken or vegetable stock (see pages 244–245)
6 Roseval red-skinned potatoes, peeled and cut into 3cm cubes
20g unsalted butter
1 radicchio cut into quarters
olive oil
1 tablespoon dried oregano
3 tablespoons anchovy paste (see page 240)
salt and pepper

Pour the stock into a large pan, add the potatoes, butter and a pinch of salt, top up with water to cover if necessary, and bring up to the boil. Turn down to a simmer and cook for 20 minutes or until the potatoes fall easily off a knife. Strain over a large bowl, keeping the cooking liquid.

Heat a charcoal Bbq (ideally) or a griddle pan to a medium heat. Rub the radicchio in olive oil, season with salt and pepper and place cut-side down on the griddle. Grill for 3 minutes then turn on to the other flat side and grill for another 3 minutes. Transfer to a bowl along with a glug of olive oil, the oregano and some salt, then cover tightly with cling film and leave the radicchio to steam in the residual heat. The cling film will inflate like a hot-air balloon; once it deflates, the radicchio's ready – roughly chop.

In a pan, on a low heat, mix together the potatoes, a little bit of their cooking liquid, the radicchio and the anchovy paste. Season with pepper and taste for salt. Add a little more potato cooking liquid if necessary – you're after an oozy consistency.

Braised hispi cabbage, clams, chilli and oregano

I love hispi cabbage in all its forms, but especially slow-cooked and smothered in buttery spicy clams.

Serves 4

2 small hispi cabbages
olive oil
1 teaspoon deseeded and finely chopped chilli
½ garlic clove, finely chopped
1 teaspoon dried oregano
½ glass white wine
200g clams (or mussels), cleaned, any open ones discarded
20g unsalted butter
pepper

Preheat the oven to 200°C/gas mark 6.

Remove the outer leaves from the cabbage and cut the cabbage in half lengthways. On a medium heat, heat some olive oil in a pan big enough to fit the length of cabbage. Working in batches, colour the cabbage on its cut side until golden. Put into a roasting tray.

Wipe away any cabbage debris from the pan and discard, then add a glug of olive oil and add the chilli, garlic and oregano. Fry for 2–3 minutes until starting to colour, then add the white wine and reduce for 3 minutes.

Transfer into the roasting tray with the cabbage and add the uncooked clams. Mix together, add a couple of centimetres of water, the butter and some pepper, then cover tightly with foil and put in the oven. Roast for 20 minutes until the cabbage is soft at the root and the clams are open (discard any closed ones). Taste to see if it needs salt (the clams might have done the job for you).

Cannellini beans, King cabbage and pancetta

This is inspired by the English classic 'bubble and squeak' – you can kinda see where I'm going, right?! This can be made in advance and kept in the fridge for up two days.

Serves 4

250g dried cannellini beans, soaked in water overnight with
    a pinch of bicarbonate of soda
½ carrot
¼ onion, peeled
½ celery stick
1 potato, peeled and roughly chopped
2 garlic cloves, finely chopped
olive oil
150–200g pancetta, cubed
1 teaspoon fennel seeds
½ teaspoon caraway seeds
2 bay leaves
juice of ½ lemon
½ cabbage (King cabbage is the best), shredded
350ml chicken stock (see page 245), or water
1 tablespoon Cabernet Sauvignon vinegar
salt and pepper

Strain and rinse the soaked cannellini beans, then put them in a casserole dish, fill with water so it's 5cm over the beans and bring to the boil. Skim off any white foam that forms and add the carrot, onion, celery, potato and garlic, plus a glug of olive oil, and simmer for 45 minutes, adding more water from time to time if the beans become exposed.

Take out a quarter of the cannellini beans, carrot and celery and roughly smash, then add back into the casserole. Discard the onion. Season with salt, pepper and olive oil.

On a medium heat, heat a glug of olive oil in a pan big enough to hold the cabbage. Add the pancetta, fennel, caraway and bay and fry for 3–4 minutes until the pancetta is starting to colour. Add the lemon juice and cabbage. Mix thoroughly, then add the chicken stock (or water), season with the vinegar, some salt (the pancetta is salty so you might not need much) and a good whack of pepper. Cover with parchment paper or a lid and cook, still on a medium heat, for 25 minutes. Combine everything together and serve.

Dijon mustard mashed potato, grilled marinated radicchio and pickled red onion

In my opinion it's impossible not to love mashed potato. Adding a dollop of Dijon mustard along with some bittersweet pickled things is like dolling it up for a night out.

Serves 4

6 mashing potatoes (such as Maris Piper), peeled and cut into
   3cm cubes
150ml milk
4 garlic cloves, peeled
6 bay leaves
30g unsalted butter
2 tablespoons Dijon mustard
salt and pepper

For the radicchio
1 radicchio, cut into quarters
olive oil
1 tablespoon dried oregano
juice and grated zest of ¼ orange,
caster sugar
salt and pepper

For the pickled red onion
150ml Cabernet Sauvignon vinegar
25ml water
½ teaspoon sugar
½ red onion, thinly sliced

First prepare the radicchio. Heat a Bbq or griddle pan to a medium heat. Rub the radicchio in olive oil, season with salt and pepper and put cut-side down on the griddle. Grill for 3 minutes then turn onto the other flat side and grill for another 3 minutes. Transfer into a bowl and add the oregano, orange zest and juice, a glug of olive oil, a tiny sprinkle of sugar and mix. Cover the bowl tightly with cling film and leave the radicchio to steam in the residual heat – the cling film will inflate like a hot-air balloon and once it deflates, the radicchio's ready! The steam helps to create a marinade. You can keep the radicchio in the fridge for a couple of days: just heat it up when you need to use it.

To make the pickled red onion, in a small pan heat up the vinegar and water. Add the sugar and leave to dissolve then take off the heat and leave to cool. Submerge the sliced onions in the vinegar mix. Leave for an hour and remove with a slotted spoon when serving.

Put the potatoes on to boil in lightly salted water for about 20 minutes. Meanwhile, heat the milk in a pan, add the garlic and bay and simmer for 15 minutes. Add the butter and remove from the heat.

The potatoes shouldn't be far off now: you need them to fall off a knife without any resistance. When they're ready, strain and mash while still hot — add the mustard and the strained buttery milk goodness a little at a time so you get the right consistency (not sloppy!). Season with salt and a good whack of pepper. Serve the pickled red onion and grilled radicchio on either side of the mash.

Roseval potato, red pepper, anchovy, olive, chilli and rosemary al forno

The potatoes won't get crispy because they absorb all of the flavours they're hanging out with, but they do get wonderfully gooey and sticky.

Serves 4

2 red peppers
olive oil
6 Roseval red-skinned potatoes, skin-on and sliced 2cm thick
3 whole salted anchovies, washed and de-boned (or use 6 good-quality fillets)
24 green or purple olives, de-stoned
½ red chilli, deseeded and finely sliced
4 garlic cloves, peeled and smashed
3 sprigs of rosemary, leaves picked
200ml chicken or vegetable stock (see pages 244–245)
2 tablespoons Cabernet Sauvignon vinegar
40g unsalted butter, cubed
salt and pepper

Preheat the oven to 190°C/gas mark 5.

Blister the peppers, ideally on a charcoal grill to get a smoky flavour, but if not, over a naked flame on a wire rack or using metal tongs – keep rolling them around until they're blackened all over. Put in a bowl and cover tightly with cling film: it will inflate like a hot-air balloon. Wait until it deflates, then peel the peppers while they're still warm (this makes it much easier). Discard the seeds and thinly slice. Put a glug of olive oil in a small saucepan and cook the peppers for 20 minutes on a low to medium heat.

Line a large, high-sided roasting tray with a thin layer of olive oil, then with parchment paper (the oil makes it stick down). Add all the ingredients (including the peppers), except the butter. Season with a big glug of olive oil, salt and a good smack of pepper, mix together and roast in the oven for 35 minutes, stirring from time to time.

Add the butter and roast for a further 5 minutes. The potatoes should have absorbed most of the liquid but have a shimmering viscous sauce.

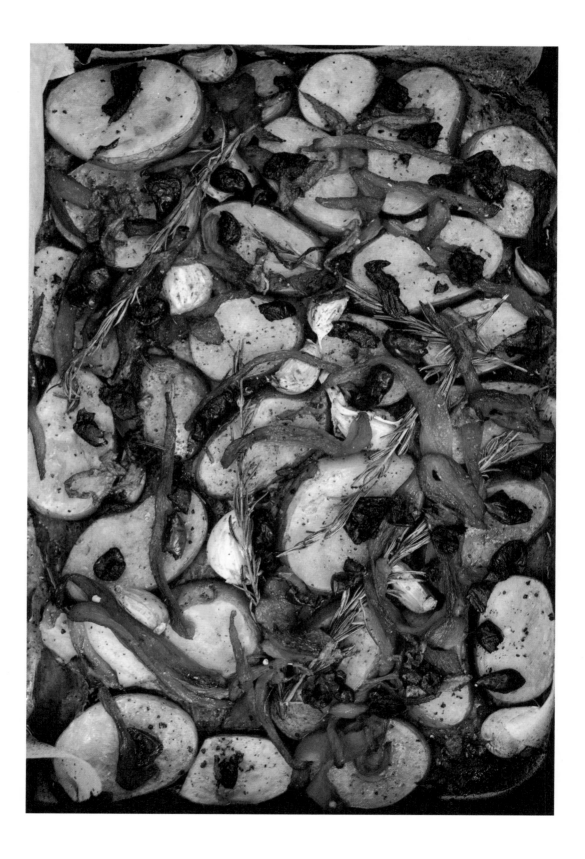

Castelluccio lentils, chopped chicken liver and fig crostini

The fruit and the liver are really lovely alongside game birds; the lentils marry the two together and make it a meal. (You could use Puy lentils if you can't get Castelluccio.) Both the liver and the lentils can be made in advance: keep in the fridge for up to two days.

Serves 4

For the lentils
olive oil
½ onion, finely chopped
1 carrot, finely chopped
½ celery stick, finely chopped
2 garlic cloves, finely chopped
4 bay leaves
500g dried Castelluccio lentils
1 tablespoon Cabernet Sauvignon vinegar, plus 1 teaspoon
10 leaves parsley, picked and finely chopped
salt and pepper

For the chicken liver and fig crostini
olive oil
½ shallot, finely chopped
4 sage leaves
4 chicken livers
75ml Marsala
100ml chicken stock (see page 245)
40g unsalted butter
4 crostini (bread cut into 8cm squares)
4 ripe figs, torn in half

To cook the lentils, heat a pan large enough to hold them on a low heat and add a glug of olive oil, the vegetables and bay leaves, but not the lentils. Sweat for 30 minutes slow and low – the natural sugars caramelise, creating a flavoursome foundation that makes all the difference to the final product. Your aim is to end up with a soft vegetal mass – if it looks as though it's starting to catch and take on too much colour, add a splash of water and take off the heat for a moment to allow the temperature to come down and then you can start again (control the heat, don't let it control you!).

Add the lentils and stir into the mix, then turn the heat up to medium and add the tablespoon of vinegar. Stir for 30 seconds, add water to cover the lentils by a couple of centimetres then cover with parchment paper, turn the heat down and simmer for 30–40 minutes. The lentils should have a tiny bite left to them. Add the parsley, a glug of olive oil, 1 teaspoon of vinegar and season with salt and pepper.

To cook the livers, first heat some olive oil in a pan on a medium to low heat and sweat the shallot and sage for 25 minutes until soft and starting to colour, then remove from the heat.

Heat a frying pan on a high heat, add a touch of olive oil and add the chicken livers. Fry hard on one side for 1½ minutes, then turn and fry for 1 minute. Add the Marsala, chicken stock and butter. Cook for a further minute and transfer immediately to a bowl to cool down. Roughly chop, add the shallots and sage and season with salt and pepper.

To serve, toast the crostinis, spread with chicken liver and smudge a fig on top. Spoon some of the hot lentils over so the crostini gets saturated in all the yummy flavours.

Runner beans, red pepper, basil and crème fraîche

For me, runner beans should only be eaten in the middle of summer when they're sweet and juicy, otherwise there really isn't any point. I love them simply tossed in butter or olive oil but here's a jazzier take for a balmy summer's night.

Serves 4

2 red peppers
a glug of olive oil
1kg runner beans, sides peeled and beans chopped into 2½cm pieces
3 tablespoons crème fraîche
10 basil leaves
juice of ¼ lemon
salt and pepper

Blister the peppers, ideally on a charcoal grill to get a smoky flavour, but if not, over a naked flame on a wire rack or using metal tongs — keep rolling the peppers around until they're blackened all over. Put them in a bowl and cover tightly with cling film: it will inflate like a hot-air balloon. Wait until it deflates, then peel the peppers when they're still warm (this makes it much easier). Discard the seeds and thinly slice.

Put a pan on a low to medium heat and add a glug of olive oil and the sliced red pepper; season with salt and cook for 25 minutes to release the natural sugars, adding a splash of water from time to time to prevent them catching.

Meanwhile, bring a large pan of water to the boil and lightly season with salt. Cook the runner beans for 5 minutes then strain.

Add the runner beans to the peppers along with the crème fraîche, basil leaves and lemon juice, and season with salt and pepper.

Stewed bobby beans

Bobby beans are a fatter, more robust version of a fine green bean and grace us around the summer months. (Our greatest ever Trullo menu typo was with a bobby bean; we didn't realise until mid-service when a customer asked for an extra-large portion of the 'booby beans' – tickles me every time!) You could use fine green beans if you can't get bobby beans.

Serves 4

a glug of olive oil
2 garlic cloves, finely chopped
¼ red chilli, finely chopped
1 tablespoon dried oregano
4 anchovy fillets
2 ripe tomatoes, roughly chopped and seeds discarded (we use ripe
    San Marzano tomatoes, but you could use any ripe tomato)
2kg bobby beans, stalks discarded

In a pan big enough to fit all the ingredients, heat a good glug of olive oil on a low heat. Add the garlic, chilli, oregano and anchovy and fry gently for 5 minutes. Add the tomatoes and continue frying for 15 minutes until everything is broken up into a happy mush.

Meanwhile, bring a large pan of water to the boil and season with salt. Add the beans, cook for 7 minutes and drain.

Add the beans to the mushy tomatoey goodness and stir. Cover with parchment paper or a lid and cook on a low heat for 35–40 minutes, stirring from time to time – add a splash of water to avoid it becoming too dry. Season with salt and pepper.

Baked borlotti beans, coco blanc or cannellini and salsa rossa/verde

Borlotti are the prettiest of beans and so very versatile. This is a fridge staple over the summer months, and also tastes good cold as a midnight munchie after the pub...

This recipe uses fresh, podded beans. If you only have dried beans then soak them overnight in water with a touch of bicarbonate of soda and cook for twice as long, or until soft.

Serves 4

250g borlotti, coco blanc or cannellini beans, podded
1 tomato
½ carrot, cut into large chunks
½ celery stick, cut into large chunks
3 bay leaves and 3 sprigs of thyme, tied into a bundle with string
olive oil
2 garlic cloves, finely chopped
1 sprig of rosemary, finely chopped
8 mint leaves, finely chopped
10 parsley leaves, finely chopped
salsa rossa or verde, to serve (see page 239)

Preheat oven to 200°C/gas mark 6.

Put the beans, tomato, carrot, celery and herb bundle into a roasting tray. Mix around and squash the tomato then add a glug of olive oil and enough water to cover everything by a couple of centimetres. Cover tightly with foil (make sure there are no rips in it); give it a head start by putting it on a high heat on the stove for 3 minutes and then put it in the oven for 25 minutes.

Take the foil off the roasting tray, increase the heat up to 220°C/gas mark 7 and bake until a crust starts to form. Stir the crust into the beans and continue baking to form another crust; repeat once more.

Take all the vegetables and a quarter of the beans out and coarsely smash. Add back to the rest of the beans, discard the herb bundle and check for seasoning.

Heat a glug of olive oil in a small pan, add the chopped garlic and rosemary and fry until the garlic starts to turn golden. At this moment pour them into the beans and fold in, along with the chopped mint and parsley. Serve with a tablespoon or two of your preferred salsa.

Chapter 6:
Feasting

Feasting

When I was a child, arriving at Granny June's house was always exciting because I just knew we were about to consume something delicious: homemade lemonade with the perfect balance of sugar to zing, or a slice of Victoria sponge as light and fluffy as a cloud. I'd get hit with the familiar waft of beef dripping from the kitchen as I ran towards her, going in for a squidgy cuddle, face first into her pinny stained with lard, marge and gravy splodges.

Granny June grew absolutely everything and would constantly send me out to her garden to pick apples for crumble, dig up potatoes to roast, cut a cauliflower to be smothered in cheese, or pick gooseberries to be fooled. She was a master preserver and pickler, a cake-maker and baker; she liked to steam a pudding and wasn't afraid of butter. When you went to Granny June's, you'd often leave with cake and always with jam of some description – not the usual suspects either: plum or damson jam, or bramble jelly.

At Granny June's the dining room table was polished, the silverware sparkled, china shimmered and crystal twinkled. The placemats were homemade rectangular pieces of glass with butterflies and wild flowers pressed between them. The claret was always decanted. That's just how she rolled. Granny June was one of those old-school grannies who don't give a monkey's. She ate and drank whatever she wanted; she didn't really think about it. Most of all, she could create feasts!

It's the Sunday roasts I remember more than anything. Rather than having to coordinate all the garnishes and have everything heating on pots at the same time and then serving it all while it was hot, she'd get quite a lot of stuff made maybe half an hour before we ate, then put it into the heated service trolley that was on this extendable cord that could fit in the kitchen. (It was always a bit of a palaver because she had to connect the extendable bit into another extendable bit that would wheel all the way out to the dining room table...) On top of it all was a little thing that you could carve on, with an electric carver. I think the electric carver was a thing of the 1980s – like a lot of other random kitchen equipment – because I haven't really seen it since. I remember that heated trolley vividly, always filling up with goodies as the afternoon progressed. I'd look in there and get excited about what was going on, whether it was creamed leeks, cabbage or custard... things that can retain their heat a bit. The trolley was a big thing.

I must have only been about six or seven when I first saw Granny June make her gravy, but I remember thinking, 'that's different to how Mum does it', because I'd been used to commercial cubes. Her glasses would fog up as she leaned over a big roasting tray with all the veg she'd mirepoixed in it, and she'd go in with spoons of cornflour and homemade stock. I always remember her pouring red wine in, and then filling her glass up and drinking some at the same time. She'd take her time to get all the lumps out. Her gravy was always the best.

She would shout out to rally the troops and for someone to carve, sending the dogs into a frenzy. We would all sit down and do one big 'cheers!', signalling that lunch was on! Sunday afternoons in Carshalton were happy days and where feasting began for me. I just wish Granny June was here now so I could repay the fun.

Jordan and I first became friends over a dinner table many years ago, when he came round for dinner to the flat I was living in with his cousin. Since that first meal (braised chicken in milk), we've had many feasts and lots of laughter: it's one of our favourite pastimes and a big part of why we opened Trullo.

Whole salt beef shin, carrots, kohlrabi, potato and pearà (bone marrow and black pepper bread sauce)

A classic dish from the northern regions of Italy, bollito misto is up there in my top five meals. When eaten in the right restaurant, it's a lavish affair where the chef wheels a trolley to your table and carves an array of boiled meats in front of you – it's full on and awesome!

This is inspired by those experiences and is a killer Sunday lunch or evening supper. Shin is relatively cheap as beef goes, but requires slow and low cooking. You can choose your vegetables – I like to use carrots, kohlrabi and potatoes, but you could substitute swede, turnips, marrow...

Serves 6

2.2 kg beef shin
4 large or 8 medium carrots, peeled
4 kohlrabi, peeled and halved
4 potatoes, peeled and halved
pearà (see page 241), with amendment given below.
10 parsley leaves, finely chopped

For the brine
8 litres water
300g muscavardo sugar
100g caster sugar
600g fine sea salt
1 tbsp saltpeter, to retain colour (optional)
5 bay leaves
15 black peppercorns
10 juniper berries
4 flakes mace

To make the brine, bring 8 litres of water to the boil and add the brine ingredients. Let the sugar and salt dissolve, then turn down to a simmer for 10 minutes. Allow to cool. Add the beef shin and cover, then store in the fridge for 3–4 days.

Take the beef shin out of the brine and rinse under cold water for 5 minutes. Put it in a pan large enough to hold the vegetables as well later, cover with water and bring up to the boil, then turn down to a simmer. Simmer for 4 hours on a low heat, skimming from time to time and adding water to keep the shin totally submerged. By the end of the cooking time, you want to be able to stick a skewer in the thickest section of the meat and pull it out with no resistance.

At this point, add the vegetables and continue cooking for 30–40 minutes or until soft.

Make the perà (bone marrow, black pepper and bread sauce) as instructed on page 241, but use the beef poaching stock instead of chicken stock.

Place the beef shin and boiled vegetables on a large platter, with a big bowl of bone marrow, black pepper and bread sauce on the side. Sprinkle the parsely over the beef.

Steamed and roasted duck legs with black rice, chickpeas and marinated apricot

This is quite a lavish meal and sure to impress at a dinner party. It's a little more adventurous on the cooking side but well worth it.

Serves 4

4 duck legs
500g dried chickpeas, soaked in water overnight with a pinch of
　bicarbonate of soda
1 carrot, cut in half
1 onion, peeled and cut in half
4 garlic cloves, peeled
2 sprigs of rosemary
olive oil
juice of 2 oranges
3 bay leaves
2 tablespoons sweet onions (see page 56)
250g black rice
500ml chicken stock (see page 245), plus a 30ml ladle for the apricots
2 tablespoons Cabernet Sauvignon vinegar, plus a splash for
　the apricots
12 leaves flat-leaf parsley, finely chopped
4 apricots, halved and de-stoned
20g unsalted butter
salt and pepper

For marinating the meat
1 teaspoon demerara sugar
½ cinnamon stick, whizzed to dust
¼ nutmeg, finely grated
finely grated zest of ½ orange
salt and pepper

To make the marinade, mix together the sugar, cinnamon, nutmeg, orange zest and some salt and pepper. Smother this over the duck legs and leave to marinate in the fridge for 24–48 hours.

Strain the soaked chickpeas and rinse for a minute under cold water. Put in a pan and totally cover with water, bring up to the boil and ladle off any white foam that forms. Add the vegetables, rosemary and a glug of olive oil and simmer for 1 hour 20 minutes, until soft. Discard the vegetables and rosemary and season with salt. Meanwhile, preheat the oven to 150°C/gas mark 2.

Using a roasting tray big enough for the duck legs, pour in the orange juice then add the bay leaves and some water – you need around 2½cm of liquid in the bottom of the tray. Place a rack big enough to hold the duck legs inside the roasting tray. Season the marinated duck with salt and put on top. Cover tightly with foil and put into the preheated oven – it's vital there are no rips in the foil otherwise the duck won't cook correctly. Cook for 1½ hours.

Remove the tray from the oven and turn the heat up to 210°C/gas mark 6½. Take the foil off and pour all of the liquid into something tall and thin (this makes it easier to skim off the fat once cooled), and return the duck to the oven, uncovered, for 20 minutes or until golden and crisp. Once the duck liquid has cooled down, discard the fat.

Towards the last 30 minutes of the duck's cooking time, put the sweet onions into a pan large enough for the rice and chickpeas later, and put on a low to medium heat. Add the rice and stir, then add the chicken stock, entirely cover with a circle of parchment paper and simmer for 25 minutes adding more liquid if it gets dry. Stir in the chickpeas for the last 5 minutes.

Take the rice off the heat, add the vinegar and a glug of olive oil, season with salt and pepper and fold in the parsley. Then leave to sit for a few minutes with a lid or plate on top.

Heat a frying pan on a low to medium heat. Smother the apricot halves in olive oil, season with salt and pepper, then add to the pan cut-side down. Fry for 3 minutes, then add a splash of vinegar, a ladle of chicken stock and the butter. Turn the heat up high and reduce the liquid for 1½ minutes, then take off the heat.

Heat the duck juices.

To plate up, get 4 individual warm plates ready – you could serve it on platters, but visually this looks pretty great plated up. Serve rice and chickpeas on one side of the plate with the duck leg sitting half on and half off, duck gravy over each leg, apricots in the bullseye of the plate and their juices on top.

Whole baked turbot with poached leeks and aioli

Considering how little preparation this requires, it's amazing how extravagant it is. Serve in the roasting tray: it look cool and minimises washing-up, too.

At certain times of the year, you might be lucky enough to have roe inside your turbot. Carefully pull the roe out before cooking the fish – they are delicious gently fried in a bit of butter for 3 minutes. Add lemon juice, parsley and salt and pepper at the end, and serve on toast.

> Serves 4
>
> olive oil
> 4 sprigs of dried bunched oregano, or 1 tablespoon dried oregano
> 1 whole turbot, about 2.5–3kg, gutted and scaled
> 1.5 litres fish stock (see page 244) – you could use water but
>   it won't be as flavoursome
> 8 leeks, washed and tops trimmed
> aioli (see page 241)
> 1 lemon, cut into quarters
> salt and pepper

Make the aioli (see page 241).

Preheat the oven to 190°C/gas mark 5.

Take a roasting tray big enough to hold the turbot and line with parchment paper, smear with olive oil and season with a layer of salt, pepper and some of the oregano (this will season the underside of the fish). Lay the turbot white-side down in the tray and season the top (grey side) with another drizzle of olive oil and some salt and pepper. Lay the oregano sprigs on top (if using) or sprinkle over the rest. Roast for 25 minutes. Check if it is cooked by inserting a knife into the thickest meat, towards the head – the flesh should fall away easily and the meat should be white to the bone.

Meanwhile, in a large pan, bring the stock up to the boil and then turn down to a simmer. Add a pinch of salt, a glug of olive oil (this gives the leeks a lovely, olive-flavoured shimmer), add the leeks and cook for 20 minutes or until totally soft. You could do this the day before and reheat to serve.

Remove the leeks with a slotted spoon and put them on a warm serving plate, and spoon a small amount of stock on top. Serve the turbot in its roasting tray and the aioli in a small bowl, accompanied by lemon quarters.

Chopped beef fillet, anchovy, parmesan and melted gruyère

Years ago, our first foray into selling food was a burger stand on the Thames in Putney for the famous Oxford vs Cambridge boat race; cunningly, we named the stand 'Oarsome Burgers' (I know...!). We made a couple of quid that day – well, enough for a few pints that night – and although I will never put a burger on the menu at Trullo, this recipe pays homage to our first ever business venture!

Serves 4

500g beef fillet (ask your butcher to trim it for you)
3 tablespoons anchovy paste (see page 240)
4 tablespoons finely grated parmesan (preferably aged at least 3 years)
1 free-range or organic egg yolk
a dash of olive oil
4 slices gruyère cheese (get the best quality possible)
4 Little Gem leaves
4 buns of your choice
garnishes, optional
salt and pepper

Make the anchovy paste on page 240.

With a sharp knife, coarsely chop the beef fillet into pieces about ½cm – this gives a different texture to mincing. Put into a mixing bowl, along with the anchovy paste, parmesan, egg yolk and some salt and pepper, and mix together thoroughly. Divide into 4 and shape into burger patties.

Heat a Bbq, grill, griddle or frying pan over a medium heat, add a dash of olive oil and start to cook the burgers. Cook for 2 minutes and turn over, then cook for 1 minute more. Turn off the heat, or remove from the heat, add a slice of gruyère to each patty and allow the residual heat to melt the cheese. Meanwhile, toast the buns.

Put a leaf of Little Gem on each bun bottom, then add the burgers and whatever garnish floats your boat.

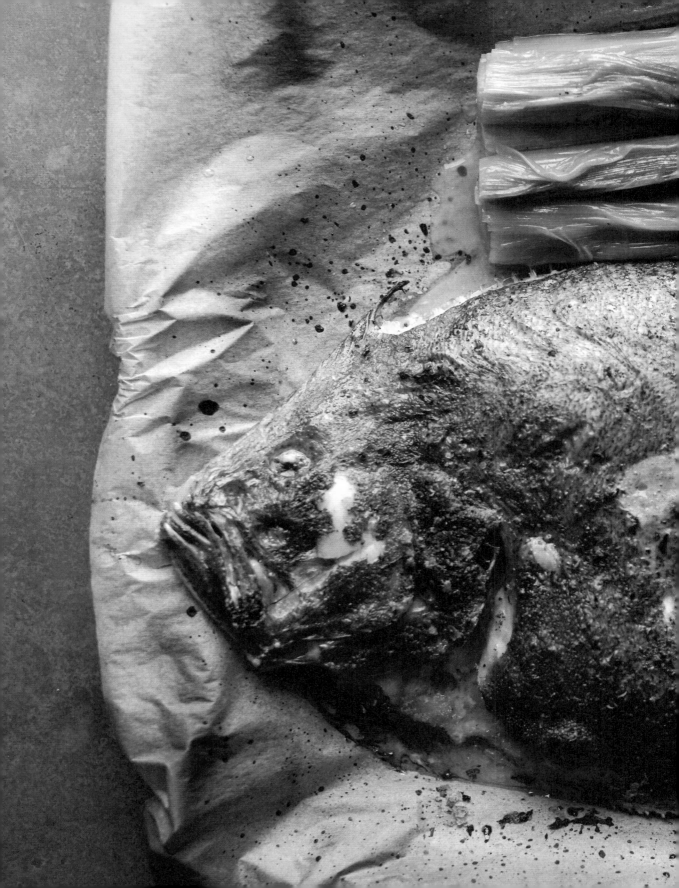

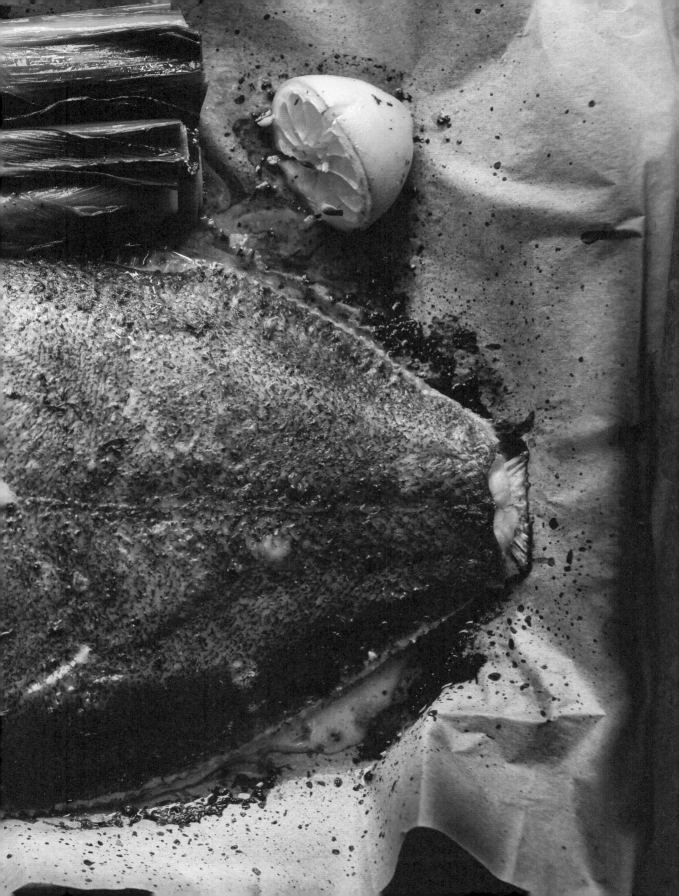

Crespelle with pumpkin, sweet onion and taleggio

Crispy pancake on the outside, sweet pumpkin and cheesy goodness in the middle. Serve with a bitter leaf salad with mustard dressing and bulk out with a pulse if you want more substance.

Serves 4

olive oil
1.2kg Crown Prince squash (or butternut squash), unpeeled but
  deseeded and cut into wedges
½ tablespoon powdered cinnamon, whizzed from a stick
¼ teaspoon ground dried chilli
5 sprigs of marjoram, leaves picked
sugar
2 tablespoons sweet onions (see page 56)
2 tablespoons grated parmesan
200g kale, steamed or boiled and roughly chopped
120g taleggio, divided into four 30g pieces
salt and pepper

For the crespelles
1 litre milk
6 free-range or organic eggs
500g flour, sifted
50g unsalted butter
olive oil
salt

Preheat the oven to 180°C/gas mark 4.

Spread a thin layer of oil in a roasting tray big enough to hold the pumpkin, and line it with parchment paper.

In a bowl, mix together the pumpkin wedges, cinnamon and chilli, some olive oil, majoram and a sprinkling of sugar, salt and pepper, then tumble into the roasting tray and add a splash of water. Roast for 1 hour or until totally soft. Remove from the oven and leave to steam dry and cool, but do not turn the oven off.

Scoop the pumpkin flesh out of its skin and put in a mixing bowl; mix in the sweet onions, parmesan and kale and season with salt and pepper.

To make the crespelle, whisk together the milk, eggs and a pinch of salt in a bowl and leave to rest for 5 minutes. Incorporate the flour slowly until a batter is formed. Heat a non-stick frying pan (around 30cm diameter) on a low to medium heat, add a knob of butter (around 10g) and a small splash of olive oil and once the butter has melted add a layer of crespelle batter to form a pancake (about 3mm thick). Cook for 2 minutes, turn and cook for a further 2 minutes, then take out of the pan. Swab the pan with kitchen paper and repeat the process until you've made 4 pancakes.

Turn the oven up to 190°C/gas mark 5.

Lay the pancakes on a clean surface. In the centre of each one, dollop a quarter of the pumpkin filling and top with a slab of taleggio, then fold the sides in to create a square parcel. Heat a large frying pan on a low to medium heat, add the remaining butter and a glug of olive oil, then add the crespelles folded-side down and fry for 2 minutes. Turn over and fry for a further 2 minutes then put in the oven for 8 minutes. Remove from the oven, transfer to kitchen paper to absorb any excess oil, and serve.

Rosemary and gorgonzola dolce farinata with yellow pepper, aubergine and courgette

Farinata is a chickpea-flour pancake from Italy's Liguria and Tuscany regions. Whenever we put this on the menu at Trullo, it ends up being the most popular dish, and I'm not surprised because it's bloody delicious.

Ideally use fresh-ground chickpea flour and always use the highest quality you can. In the UK, Asian or Middle Eastern shops tend to have the best flour (called gram flour).

Serves 4

olive oil
2 aubergines, sliced into ½ cm rounds
2 yellow peppers, deseeded and sliced into 1cm pieces
12 Datterini tomatoes
2 courgettes, sliced lengthways into ½ cm strips
2 garlic cloves, finely chopped
2 tablespoons Cabernet Sauvignon vinegar
1 tablespoon capers, salt rinsed off and capers soaked
  in water for 20 minutes
6 mint leaves
6 basil leaves
vegetable oil
6 teaspoons gorgonzola dolce per farinata pancake

For the farinata batter
500ml water
235g chickpea flour, sifted
a dash of olive oil
1 teaspoon chopped rosemary
a pinch of salt

Preheat the oven to 190°C/gas mark 5.

Heat a Bbq, griddle or frying pan on a medium heat until hot, and line a roasting tray with parchment paper. Working in batches, add some olive oil and the vegetables to the Bbq, griddle or frying pan and colour for 2 minutes on each side, then transfer into the prepared roasting tray.

Add the vinegar, the capers, a glug of olive oil and some salt and pepper, then roast in the oven for 45 minutes.

Meanwhile, make the farinata batter. Pour the water into a large mixing bowl and whisk in the chickpea flour. Add a dash of olive oil, the rosemary and a pinch of salt, then leave to rest for 30 minutes at room temperature.

Remove the roasting tray from the oven and turn the oven up to 200°C/gas mark 6. Allow the vegetables to cool then add the mint and basil and season.

You will need a non-stick frying pan (or several) that can go in the oven. For a pancake for 1 person, a 20cm pan is the perfect diameter. Heat the frying pan(s) on a medium to high heat then when hot add a ½cm layer of vegetable oil. Pour in 110ml of batter, let it bubble for 30 seconds then put the pan(s) in the oven for 3 minutes. Remove and turn the farinata over, then return to the oven for 4 minutes or until crispy. Transfer onto kitchen paper to absorb any excess fat. Repeat to make the remaining pancakes.

Add the gorgonzola dolce to one half of each farinata in small blobs. Put the farinatas into a roasting tray and return to the oven for 2 minutes until the cheese has started to melt.

Take the farinatas out of the oven, fold them in half and cut into wedges. Serve wedges of farinata with the room-temperature veg on individual plates.

Lamb, offal, orzo, purple olive and toasted pine nut meatballs with spicy tomato sauce and aubergine

Please, for the love of God, do not use standard lamb mince: go to the butcher and ask them to mince the combination below and roughly chop the offal. There's a bit going on here but it's darned good!

Serves 4

2 onions, thinly sliced
olive oil
500ml chicken stock (see page 245)
4 aubergines
Cabernet Sauvignon vinegar
6 tablespoons spicy tomato sauce (see page 107)
2 handfuls of rocket
salt

For the soffritto
a dash of olive oil
3 shallots, finely chopped
2 garlic cloves, finely chopped
20g pine nuts, coarsely chopped
1 tablespoon fennel seeds, ground
½ cinnamon stick, whizzed into a powder
1 teaspoon finely chopped rosemary

For the meatballs
500g lamb mince (a mix of shoulder, belly and leg)
300g chopped offal (a mix of lamb heart, liver and kidney)
grated zest of ½ orange
15 purple olives, de-stoned and roughly chopped
125g orzo (uncooked weight), cooked as per packet instructions
350g caul fat (also known as crépine)
salt and pepper

First, make the soffritto. On a low heat, pour a dash of olive oil into a pan and add the soffritto vegetables and flavourings, and sweat until soft and translucent – about 20 minutes.

Meanwhile, in a separate pan, sweat the sliced onions with a tiny amount of olive oil until soft and translucent; add the chicken stock and take off the heat. Preheat the oven to 170°C/gas mark 3.

Mix the soffritto with all the lamb meats and offal, the orange zest, olives and orzo, and season with salt and pepper. Check the seasoning by making a tiny patty, frying, and tasting it. Shape the mixture into meatballs about the size of a tennis ball. Cut the caul fat into pieces big enough to wrap around each meatball, then place each meatball in the middle of a piece and wrap it around.

Place the meatballs in a casserole dish or deep roasting tray so that they fit snugly, then add the chicken stock and sliced onions, cover with a lid or tightly cover with foil, and put in the oven for 1 hour 20 minutes.

Meanwhile, cut the aubergines into large chunks of around 6cm, season with salt and leave in a colander for 30 minutes to draw out some of the liquid. Pat the aubergines dry and heat a frying pan on a low to medium heat, add a thin layer of olive oil and fry until golden then transfer into a roasting tray. Add 50ml of water, drizzle with olive oil and cover tightly with foil then roast in the oven for 30 minutes, or until soft. When done, take the foil off and season with fine salt and dribble a couple of drops of vinegar on each aubergine.

Heat the tomato sauce, then mix in the rocket and take off the heat.

To serve, put some aubergine on each plate and spoon over the tomato sauce; put a meatball on the other side of the plate and spoon over the onion gravy.

Roast chicken thighs and nduja with rosemary potatoes and anchovy mayonnaise

Holy moly, this is finger-lickin' goooood! Sometimes we make it for staff food, which is basically a family meal – everyone goes bananas for it.

Serves 6

2 tablespoons nduja
8 Maris Piper potatoes, cut into wedges
4 sprigs of rosemary
6 garlic cloves, smashed
olive oil
18 chicken thighs (3 per person)
salt

For the anchovy mayonnaise
2 free-range or organic egg yolks
3 salted anchovy fillets, finely chopped
400ml groundnut oil, or other neutral oil
1 teaspoon red wine vinegar
salt and pepper

Preheat the oven to 180°C/gas mark 4.

Put the nduja in a bowl, add a splash of hot water and mix to loosen.

Put the potatoes, rosemary and a sprinkle of salt in a pan and cover with water. Bring up to the boil then drain immediately. Let the potatoes completely steam dry then coat generously with olive oil and mix together. Heat an empty roasting tray (large enough to hold the potato wedges in a single layer) in the oven for 5 minutes, then take it out and add olive oil so that it is about 3cm deep. Add the potatoes, rosemary and garlic and season with salt and pepper. Roast the potatoes on the top shelf of the oven for 45 minutes–1 hour or until crispy, stirring from time to time.

While your potatoes are roasting, heat a large frying pan on a low to medium heat. Add a small amount of olive oil. Season the chicken thighs with salt and pepper and, working in batches, colour them in the pan until golden then transfer to a roasting tray.

Put the chicken on the lower shelf of the oven and roast for the remaining time of the potatoes (roughly 30 minutes). Add the nduja for the last 15 minutes of cooking and muddle it all around.

To make the mayonnaise, put the egg yolks and anchovies in a bowl and whisk. Slowly start pouring in groundnut oil in a thin stream while whisking; continue until it has emulsified (all come together in a single mass), at which point you can start pouring a little faster – not too quickly though, otherwise it will split! Add the red wine vinegar and season with salt and pepper.

Serve the chicken and potatoes on platters in the middle of the table with a green salad.

Braised lamb shoulder, Jersey Royals, peas and mint sauce

This is a one-pot wonder and can be made the day before and reheated in the oven – perfect for a Sunday lunch in spring.

Serves 6

2.5kg whole lamb shoulder on the bone
6 shallots, peeled
12 garlic cloves, peeled
2 sprigs of rosemary
3 bay leaves
15 mint leaves, finely chopped
1 glass (125ml) white wine
1 litre chicken stock (see page 245)
500g peas, fresh or frozen
36 Jersey Royals, cleaned
salt

For the mint sauce
25ml water
60ml red wine vinegar
15g caster sugar
15 mint leaves, finely chopped

Heat a large, heavy-bottomed roasting tray big enough to hold the lamb shoulder, peas and potatoes, and colour the skin of the lamb in the tray on a low to medium heat for about 25 minutes until totally golden (tongs are useful here). It's very important to do this; partly for depth of flavour and also to render some fat. Meanwhile, preheat the oven to 160°C/gas mark 2½.

Transfer the lamb onto a plate. Discard most of the rendered fat from the roasting tray, but keep a thin layer. In the same tray, colour the shallots and garlic until golden all over, then add the herbs. Deglaze with the white wine and reduce for 5 minutes. Add the chicken stock and bring to the boil.

Transfer the lamb back into the roasting tray and nestle it on top; it needs to be three-quarters covered by liquid – if it's not, add some water. Season with salt and pepper. Cover with parchment paper, then tightly seal with foil – the paper prevents the foil sticking on the lamb, and it's crucial not to tear the foil as this will allow the steam to escape and the lamb won't cook evenly. Slow roast for 2½ hours.

Take the roasting tray out of the oven (but do not turn the oven off), remove the foil and parchment paper, add the peas and Jersey Royals and let gravity do its thing. Season the new arrivals with a pinch of salt, add a dash of water if needed and repeat the process of tightly covering with parchment and foil. Slow roast for another 2½ hours or until the meat is completely falling off the bone.

To make the mint sauce, boil the water and vinegar in a pan, turn down the heat and stir in the sugar until dissolved. Allow to cool to room temperature then add the mint and stir together.

I serve the lamb in the roasting tray in the middle of the table.

Beef T-bone, wild mushrooms and Marsala with deep-fried polenta and gorgonzola fonduta

Whether it's for a date night, bromance or girls' night in, this is outrageously opulent. There are rules to this dish though: you must buy well aged, good-quality beef; if you drink alcohol, for love of God get decent Barolo, Chianti or Montalcino (or similar); and don't use instant polenta that cooks in three minutes – in fact you should never use it! It's not the same product as the proper stuff.

This is nice served with a bitter leaf salad with mustard dressing.

Serves 2–3

800ml water
130g polenta
900g T-bone
1.25 litres rapeseed oil, for frying (for a 20cm diameter pan)
4 tablespoons gorgonzola dolce
1 tablespoon crème fraîche
10 parsley leaves, finely chopped
salt and pepper

For the mushrooms
a glug of olive oil
1 garlic clove, finely chopped
100g mixed wild mushrooms (porcini, chanterelle, girolle and morels), dirt and soil removed with a damp tissue or pastry brush – be gentle!
50ml Marsala
200ml chicken stock (see page 245)
40g unsalted butter

First make the polenta. Pour the water into a large pan and add some salt. Bring to the boil and add the polenta in a stream, whisking continually for the first 2 minutes. Turn down to a simmer and cook for 40 minutes. Check for seasoning and turn out onto a dish with sides that come up at least 3cm then leave to cool down. Put in the fridge to chill and firm up. Tear the firm polenta into large bite-sized pieces and pat dry.

To prepare the mushrooms, heat a frying pan on a medium heat, then add a glug of olive oil and the garlic. Fry for 1 minute until the garlic is just starting to go golden then add the mushrooms and sauté for 2 minutes. Add the Marsala, reduce for 1 minute then add the chicken stock and butter and reduce until the sauce has emulsified and is viscous. Put to one side.

Preheat a Bbq or griddle pan to a medium heat. Meanwhile, season the T-bone with salt and leave for 20 minutes (out of the fridge). This not only seasons the meat and brings it up to temperature but you'll also see that it draws out some liquid, which forms a better seal when added to the heat, creating more flavour.

Put your T-bone on the grill or griddle, seal on one side for 3 minutes, then turn over and cook for 3 minutes more. Turn on to the fat side and colour and render until golden. If you want your steak rare, take it off the heat now. If not, continue to cook, turning every minute or so. Increments of 3 minutes extra will take it into other cuissons (medium rare, medium, medium well, well done). Leave to rest in a warm tray for 10 minutes.

While cooking the steak, heat the frying oil to 180°C.

Reheat the mushrooms and their liquid until hot. In a separate pan, heat the gorgonzola and crème fraîche on a low heat until it has all combined into a creamy fonduta.

While your steak is resting, add the polenta pieces to the hot oil and fry until crispy and golden (about 4 minutes) then place in a bowl lined with kitchen paper and season with salt.

To serve, place the T-bone on a board and cut off the meat either side of the bone. Slice crossways into thin strips. Put the bone on a large, hot plate and lay slices of steak back into position around the bone. Season with salt and lots of pepper and pour the mushrooms and liquid on top. Put the polenta in a serving dish, pour the gorgonzola fonduta on top and sprinkle with chopped parsley.

Rolled pork loin stuffed with nduja and prunes with chickpeas, red pepper, spinach and rosemary

Sweet sticky prunes and spicy nduja running through the core of the loin may sound a little unusual but trust me, it takes the pork to glorious new heights. It's also delicious sliced super-thin when cold.

Serves 6

3 red peppers
olive oil
1kg spinach
1.75kg pork loin (unrolled)
6 tablespoons nduja
20 prunes, de-stoned and roughly chopped
8 bay leaves
1 pig trotter (optional), slashed with a knife then washed
3 red onions, thinly sliced
8 tablespoons Cabernet Sauvignon vinegar
400ml chicken stock (see page 245)
salt and pepper

For the chickpeas
1kg dried chickpeas, soaked in water overnight with a teaspoon
  of bicarbonate of soda
1 carrot, cut in half
1 onion, peeled and chopped in half
1 celery stick
4 bay leaves
3 sage leaves
olive oil
2 garlic cloves, finely chopped
3 sprigs of rosemary, leaves picked

First prepare the chickpeas: drain them of their soaking water and rinse for a minute under cold water. Add to a pan and totally cover with water, then bring up to the boil and ladle off any white foam that forms. Add the carrot, onion, celery, bay, sage and a glug of olive oil and simmer for 1 hour 20 minutes until soft.

Discard the vegetables and herbs, then take out a quarter of the chickpeas and about 50ml of liquid and whizz into a paste. Add this back to the rest of the chickpeas. Heat some oil in a small pan and fry the garlic and rosemary until just golden, then stir into the chickpeas to stop the garlic from cooking.

Blister the peppers, ideally on a charcoal grill to get a smoky flavour, but if not, over a naked flame on a wire rack or using metal tongs – keep rolling them around until they're blackened all over. Put in a bowl and cover tightly with cling film. The film will inflate like a hot-air balloon; once it comes back down, peel the peppers. Do this while they're still warm as it's much easier.

Discard the seeds from the peppers, thinly slice and put in a saucepan on a medium to low heat. Add a glug of olive oil, season with salt and cook for 25 minutes to release the natural sugars, adding a splash of water from time to time to prevent them from catching. Steam or boil the spinach, and once cooked squeeze out the excess liquid. Preheat the oven to 180°C/gas mark 4.

Lay the pork loin on a large chopping board, fat-side down. You need to butterfly the meat: this basically means you even out the meat so it is roughly the same thickness throughout. Get a sharp knife and cut into the fatter/meatier areas to level it out.

In a mixing bowl, mix the nduja with a touch of hot water and a dash of olive oil. Add the prunes and mix again. Spread over the flesh of the meat and season with salt and pepper.

There are fancier ways of tying joints of meat but if you're not experienced, simple individual knots do the job. Roll the loin up tightly and start to tie the ends first, then the middle and then in the gaps. If you loop twice before you tie each knot, you'll find it stays in place without you having to hold it tight.

Heat a heavy-bottomed frying pan or roasting tray on a medium to low heat, season the rolled loin with salt and pepper, then add a glug of olive oil to the tray and brown the loin. Take your time to get a golden colour all around the fat (this is flavour), rolling it with a pair of tongs – this will take about 10–15 minutes.

Remove the loin and add the bay leaves, pig trotter (if using) and red onions, and cook on a low heat for 10–15 minutes until the onions are softened. Put the loin back in, then the vinegar, followed by 200ml chicken stock or water; cover with parchment paper and tightly seal with foil. Pot-roast for 1½ hours.

Take the loin out to rest for 15–20 minutes. Meanwhile, add about 200ml chicken stock to the roasting tray and leave to soak to create a gravy. While the loin is resting, mix together the chickpeas, peppers and spinach in a pan on a medium heat. Add water if it needs loosening, and a dash of olive oil to gloss it up, then season with salt and pepper.

Carve the pork into slices no thicker than 1cm, set out on a hot platter and spoon gravy on top. Serve the chickpeas, pepper and spinach in a bowl.

Chapter 7:
Sauces & stocks

Sauces

Salsa verde

There are hundreds of recipes for salsa verde, and you can play around with any soft herbs. I add Dijon mustard when using it with pork, beef and game.

Serves 6

30 mint leaves
30 parsley leaves
30 tarragon leaves
300ml olive oil
1 tablespoon coarsely chopped cornichons
1 teaspoon roughly chopped good-quality anchovy fillets
1 teaspoon capers, salt rinsed off and soaked in water for 20 minutes, then finely chopped
½ garlic clove, minced
1 tablespoon Cabernet Sauvignon vinegar
salt and pepper

Finely chop the herbs then quickly submerge in the olive oil to prevent oxidisation. Stir in all the other ingredients and season with salt and pepper.

Salsa rossa (summer)

Serves 6

1 red pepper
300ml olive oil
15 red chillies, deseeded and finely chopped
8 Datterini tomatoes, blanched in boiling water for 45 seconds
   then peeled, deseeded and finely chopped
1 teaspoon Cabernet Sauvignon vinegar
½ teaspoon minced garlic
salt and pepper

Blacken the red pepper on a Bbq or over a naked flame on a wire rack or using metal tongs. Transfer into a bowl and cover with cling film; the film will inflate like a hot-air balloon. When it deflates, peel and deseed the pepper.

Cut the pepper into strips, put them in a small pan with a touch of olive oil and cook for 30 minutes on a low heat, stirring from time to time.

Roughly chop the cooked pepper strips, put in a bowl with the remaining oil and all the other ingredients and mix. Season with salt and pepper.

Salsa rossa (all year)

Serves 6

2 tablespoons torn-up sourdough bread
1 tablespoon Cabernet Sauvignon vinegar
20 red chillies, deseeded and finely chopped
½ teaspoon sweet paprika
½ teaspoon minced garlic
300ml olive oil
salt and pepper

In a bowl, soak the bread in the vinegar for 20 minutes and break up into a mush. Add all the remaining ingredients and mix. Season with salt and pepper.

Anchovy paste

Makes ½ litre

100g good-quality anchovy fillets
½ teaspoon minced garlic
400ml olive oil
1 teaspoon red wine vinegar
salt and pepper

Put the anchovies and garlic in a food processor and whizz. Slowly pour in the olive oil until a thick paste is formed; add 3–4 tablespoons cold water and the vinegar – it should be easily spreadable, add water if not. Check for seasoning.

Gorgonzola fonduta

2 parts gorgonzola dolce
1 part crème fraîche

Gently heat together over a very low heat until it has all combined into a creamy sauce.

Purple olive dressing

Serves 6

36 Kalamata olives, de-stoned and coarsely chopped
1 red chilli, deseeded and finely chopped
8 flat-leaf parsley leaves, finely chopped
1 anchovy fillet, finely chopped
finely grated zest of ¼ lemon
300ml olive oil
salt and pepper

Put all the ingredients into a bowl and mix. Check for seasoning.

Pearà (bone marrow and black pepper bread sauce)

Serves 6

4 veal marrow bones, each 8cm long
250g torn-up sourdough bread
500ml chicken stock (see page 245), plus a little extra
3 tablespoons freshly ground black pepper
salt

Preheat the oven to 180°C/gas mark 4.

Roast the marrow bones for 20 minutes. When cool enough to handle, scoop the marrow into a pan and add the bread. Cook on a medium heat for a few minutes until the bread has absorbed the marrow and has broken up. Add the chicken stock and pepper and simmer on a low heat for 1½ hours. Note: as it cooks it will stick to the bottom of the pan; take the pan off the heat for 5 minutes and then scrape the bottom of the pan and mix. You may need to add a little more chicken stock or water as you go. Season to taste. The aim is to have the same consistency as normal bread sauce.

Aioli

Makes about 650ml
(enough for about 10 people)

4 free-range or organic egg yolks
1 garlic clove, minced
600ml groundnut oil, or other neutral oil
1 tablespoon red wine vinegar
salt and pepper

To make the mayonnaise, put the egg yolks and garlic in a bowl and whisk. Slowly start pouring groundnut oil in a thin stream while whisking; continue until it has emulsified (it will come together into a single mass) at which point you can start pouring a little faster – but not too quickly or it will split! Add the red wine vinegar and season with salt and pepper.

Stocks

Take pride in your stocks, they're a vital strand of excellent cooking.

Vegetable stock

Makes 4 litres

2 carrots, roughly chopped
1 onion, peeled and cut into quarters
2 celery sticks, roughly chopped
1 leek, sliced in half lengthways
4 bay leaves
8 sprigs each of thyme, rosemary and parsley
1 tablespoon fennel seeds

Put all the ingredients into a large pan, cover with 5 litres of water and bring up to the boil. Turn down to a simmer, skim off any foam that forms and simmer for 45 minutes, skimming continuously. Strain, discard all the solid ingredients and pour the stock back into the pan. Bring to the boil and reduce the stock to 4 litres.

Fish stock

Makes 4 litres

1kg cleaned white fish bones
1 onion, peeled and cut into quarters
2 celery sticks, roughly chopped
1 leek, sliced in half lengthways
4 bay leaves
8 sprigs each of thyme, rosemary and parsley
1 tablespoon fennel seeds
1 tablespoon peppercorns
½ lemon

Put the fish bones into a large pan and add 5 litres of water. Bring up to the boil, then turn down to a simmer; continuously skimming until no foam forms. Add all of the remaining ingredients and simmer for 35 minutes. Strain, discard all the solid ingredients and pour the stock back into the pan. Bring to the boil and reduce to 4 litres.

Chicken stock

Makes 4 litres

1.5kg washed chicken bones
1 onion, peeled and cut into quarters
2 celery sticks, roughly chopped
1 leek, sliced in half lengthways
4 bay leaves
8 sprigs each of thyme, rosemary, tarragon and parsley
1 tablespoon fennel seeds
1 tablespoon peppercorns

Preheat the oven to 180°C/gas mark 4. Roast the chicken bones, turning them over from time to time, until beautifully golden.

Transfer to a large pan, add 8 litres of water and bring to the boil. Turn down to a simmer and skim off any foam and fat that forms at the top. After 15 minutes, add all the remaining ingredients and simmer for 4 hours, continuously skimming off any fat that forms (a perfect stock should have no fat in it). Strain, discard all the solid ingredients and pour the stock back into the pan. Bring to the boil and reduce to 4 litres.

Chapter 8:
Desserts, ice cream
& granita

Desserts

From my teens on, always cheese, rarely dessert, was how I used to roll. But the older I've got, the sweeter my tooth has become, and although I might adamantly insist I don't want any pud, when it's there giving me the eye I feebly crumble within seconds and lunge in with a premeditated form of cutlery. The truth is, if you're a dessert fan you'll always have one and if you're not, well, you're not fussed either way.

The selection here is a mixture of Italian classics and the happy results of Trullo play-time, ranging from light and refreshing palate cleansers (like our blood orange granita, page 272), to naughty and fulfilling treats (of which tiramisu is surely the ultimate, see page 255).

If you are cooking a meal for a group, consider what sort of dessert will round everything off nicely – nobody actually likes being full to the brim.

Chilled zabaglione

Although chilled, this works just as well in the depths of winter as it does in the height of summer – up the booze quotient if you're feeling fruity.

It is really important to use high-quality fresh egg yolks.

Serves 4

16 large free-range or organic egg yolks
150g caster sugar
2 vanilla pods, slit in half lengthways and seeds scraped out
50ml Marsala
500ml double cream

In a bowl set over a saucepan of simmering water, whisk together the egg yolks, sugar, vanilla seeds and Marsala until quadrupled in size (roughly 10 minutes). Transfer into a large bowl and leave to chill in the fridge.

Whisk the cream until thick enough to form soft peaks, and fold it into the zabaglione. Serve in a glass, with fruit of your choice.

Upside-down blood orange cake

I love the contrast of the bittersweet orange caramel that forms when you turn this cake upside down paired with the dense almond sponge.

Serves 10–12

140g blanched almonds
80g soft brown sugar
75g unsalted butter, chilled and cubed, plus 175g, softened
4 blood oranges, 1 of them finely zested
335g caster sugar
1 vanilla pod, slit lengthways and seeds scraped out
3 medium free-range or organic eggs, separated
145g plain flour, sifted
2½ teaspoons baking powder
180ml milk
crème fraîche, to serve

Preheat the oven to 170C/gas mark 3.

Grind the almonds in a blender to resemble coarse crumbs.

Peel all the oranges and slice into 3mm slices, removing the seeds.

Place a 28cm spring-form tin on a baking tray. Grease with a little bit of butter or oil then line the entire tin with parchment paper. Sprinkle with the brown sugar and the cold cubed butter and put in the oven for 3 minutes until the butter has melted. Lay the orange slices over the melted butter and sugar so the base of the tin is covered.

In a mixing bowl, beat together the softened butter, orange zest, caster sugar and vanilla seeds until they double in volume and become light and fluffy. Add the egg yolks one by one while constantly beating. Add the flour, ground almonds and baking powder, slowly beating, and then gradually add the milk until a batter forms.

Whisk the egg whites to firm peaks and fold into the batter. Pour the batter over the orange slices and bake for 1½ hours.

Remove the cake from the oven and place it on a pastry rack to cool in the tin. Turn upside down on a chopping board, release the tin and carefully remove the parchment paper.

Serve with crème fraîche.

Chocolate tart

I was taught this at Moro and have yet to find a better recipe.

Serves 10

For the pastry
140g plain flour, sifted
40g icing sugar, sifted
75g unsalted butter, very cold and cubed
2 free-range or organic egg yolks, plus 1 medium, whisked, for brushing

For the chocolate filling
180g dark chocolate (70% cocoa)
250g unsalted butter
4 medium free-range or organic eggs
120g caster sugar

To make the pastry, put the flour and icing sugar in a bowl or a food processor and mix. Add the butter and combine until you have the texture of fine breadcrumbs. Add the egg yolks one at a time, continuously mixing to form a dough. Wrap in cling film and chill until firm.

Preheat the oven to 150°C/gas mark 2. (You bake the pastry at a lower temperature but for a longer time than for the almond tart on page 260, because you need a firmer crust as the chocolate mousse filling is really wet – you don't want a soggy bottom...)

Get a 24cm loose-based, non-stick tart tin and coarsely grate the pastry into the middle. Start pushing the pastry up the sides of the case with your thumbs and then form the base. Bake in the preheated oven for 28 minutes then take out, brush with whisked egg and bake for a further 8 minutes.

While the tart shell is baking, make the chocolate filling: in a heat-resistant bowl over a pan of gently simmering water, heat the chocolate and butter until they are melted, and mix together.

When the tart shell is ready, take out of the oven and turn the oven down to 130°C/gas mark ½. Whisk together the eggs and sugar for the filling until very white and quadrupled in size, and fold into the chocolate mixture. Pour into the tart shell and bake for 11 minutes. Take out and allow to cool on a pastry rack.

Tiramisu

The ultimate indulgence, and very naughty, but such a treat! This is my version of the classic we all know.

Serves 6

2 free-range or organic egg yolks
60g caster sugar
1 vanilla pod, split in half lengthways and seeds scraped out
40ml Marsala
250g mascarpone
225ml double cream
24 lady fingers
500ml cooled strong black coffee (not instant!)
good-quality cocoa powder, for dusting

In a heat-resistant bowl over a saucepan of gently simmering water, whisk together the egg yolks, caster sugar, vanilla seeds and Marsala until doubled in size and creamy, then leave to cool in the fridge.

Whisk together the mascarpone and double cream until smooth and thickened to soft peaks.

Get a small tray/dish with 4cm-high sides. One by one, soak the lady fingers in coffee for 3 seconds to absorb (don't let them go soggy) and start laying them down on the base of the dish. Spread half of the zabaglione (egg mixture) on the lady fingers then spread half of the mascarpone mixture on top of that. Repeat the entire process with the remaining lady fingers, zabaglione and mascarpone mixture, and set in the fridge until chilled.

Sprinkle with cocoa powder before serving.

Vanilla and bitter caramel pannacotta

Wibbly, wobbly and wicked. You'll need six ramekins, 10cm diameter and 8cm deep.

Serves 6

5 sheets silver gelatin
150ml cold milk
1 litre whipping cream
150g icing sugar
2 vanilla pods, slit in half lengthways and seeds scraped out
350g caster sugar

Soak the gelatin in the cold milk for 20 minutes.

To make the pannacotta, put the cream in a non-stick pan, add the icing sugar and vanilla seeds and gently bring up to a simmer, then take off the heat. Add the gelatin, pouring in the cold milk first then the soaked sheets and whisking until the gelatin dissolves. Chill in the fridge until just starting to thicken (about 45 minutes).

While the pannacotta is in the fridge, make your caramel: put the caster sugar in a non-stick pan and, on a low to medium heat, start melting it, stirring with a wooden spoon. Be very careful of the smoke and open your windows. Set out 6 ramekins and, when the sugar turns to a dark brown caramel (10–15 minutes), pour about 1cm into each ramekin and allow to firm up.

Whisk the pannacotta mixture and pour to just under the ramekin rims and leave to set in the fridge overnight.

To serve, loosen the pannacotta seal with the tip of a sharp knife, dip the ramekins halfway into a bowl of very hot water for 7 seconds, and turn out on to cold plates.

Grilled peaches with Amaretto and vanilla mascarpone

At the height of summer, white peaches are plentiful, and they're totally delicious eaten as Mother Earth intended, but this is a simple way of jazzing them up.

If you don't have white peaches to hand, any peach will work.

Serves 4

200g mascarpone
½ teaspoon vanilla seeds (from 2 vanilla pods, slit in half lengthways and seeds scraped out)
1 teaspoon icing sugar, sifted, plus 1 tablespoon, sifted
4 peaches (ideally white), cut in half and de-stoned
a little olive oil
50g unsalted butter, cubed
100ml Amaretto

Mix together the mascarpone, vanilla seeds and 1 teaspoon of icing sugar.

Preheat a Bbq, griddle or frying pan to a medium to low heat. Rub the flesh of the peaches with olive oil and sprinkle with 1 tablespoon of icing sugar then grill flesh-side down for 3 minutes. Transfer to a tray, add the butter and Amaretto, cover tightly with cling film, then leave for 15 minutes.

Remove the cling film and put two peach halves on each plate. Transfer the liquid to a pan, set on a high heat and reduce for 1 minute. To serve, pour over the peaches and spoon a dollop of vanilla mascarpone next to them.

Summer almond tart

This rarely leaves the Trullo menu, because it possesses the ability to wear many faces with different moods and always pleases.

Serves 12

For the pastry
140g plain flour, sifted
40g icing sugar, sifted
75g unsalted butter, very cold and cubed
2 free-range or organic egg yolks

For the frangipane
250g blanched almonds
250g caster sugar
250g unsalted butter, softened
3 medium free-range or organic eggs

crème fraîche, to serve

To make the pastry, put the flour and icing sugar in a bowl or a food processor and mix. Add the butter and mix until you have the texture of fine breadcrumbs. Add the egg yolks one at a time, continuously mixing to form a dough. Wrap in cling film and chill until firm.

To make the frangipane, grind or pound the almonds; I like different textures of almond so do it in three stages (coarse, medium and medium fine) taking a third out each time.

Cream the caster sugar and butter until light and fluffy; add the eggs one at a time while continuously mixing. Add the ground or pounded almonds and chill in the fridge.

Preheat the oven to 170°C/gas mark 3, and take the frangipane out of the fridge to become malleable.

Get a 26cm loose based, non-stick tart shell and coarsely grate the pastry in the middle. Start pushing the pastry up the sides of the case with your thumbs and then form the base. Bake in the preheated oven for 14 minutes, then fill the tart shell with frangipane and return to bake for 1 hour.

Leave to cool before serving with crème fraîche.

Pear and almond tart

Serves 12

1 batch pastry dough (see page 260)
1 batch frangipane (see page 260)
crème fraîche, to serve

For the poached pears
3 pears, peeled (not too ripe)
800ml water
200ml white wine
100g caster sugar
½ cinnamon stick
rind of 1 orange
rind of 1 lemon
1 vanilla pod, split in half lengthways and seeds scraped out

To poach the pears, put all the ingredients apart from the pears in a large pot and bring up to the boil. Turn down to a simmer and add the pears. Poach for 10 minutes. Take off the heat and allow the pears to cool in the liquid.

Meanwhile, prepare the pastry and frangipane (see page 260) and chill in the fridge until needed.

Once the pears have cooled, slice around the core into quarters.

Preheat the oven to 170°C/gas mark 3, and take the frangipane out of the fridge to become malleable.

Get a 26cm loose based non-stick tart shell and coarsely grate the pastry into the middle. Start pushing the pastry up the sides of the case with your thumbs and then form the base. Bake in the oven for 14 minutes.

Turn the oven down to 160°C/gas mark 2 and fill the tart shell with the frangipane. Place the pears on top, leaving some gaps, and bake for 90 minutes.

Leave to cool before serving with crème fraiche.

Ice cream

Probably above any other food, ice cream universally makes people happy. There aren't many things that have that effect on humans – ice cream, we salute you!

Included here is a short selection of my favourite flavours. All these recipes require an ice-cream maker.

Granita

Granita is a wonderful way to wrap up a heavy meal up because it's light, clean and healthy; what's more it's ridiculously easy to make. The key, when using fruits, is to be sure you use super-ripe fruit and fresh juice. Then it's a simple process of transferring the juice into a relatively flat container, freezing it and every hour or so raking it with a fork so it forms tiny little crystals (no lumps!) – that's it!

If the juice is too sweet, add some lemon juice to taste. If you want to sweeten your juice, add a little sugar syrup to taste. To make sugar syrup, just add equal parts sugar and water into a pan and set over a low heat for the sugar to dissolve, without stirring. Continue heating until reduced by half and you'll have syrup.

The granita quantities given all serve 6.

Marsala and raisin affogato

Use high-quality fresh egg yolks for ice cream.

Serves 6

50g raisins
100ml Marsala, plus 50ml for soaking the raisins, plus extra chilled
 in the freezer for serving (optional)
335ml double cream
200ml milk
1 vanilla pod, slit in half lengthways
8 free-range or organic egg yolks
100g caster sugar
6 espressos, or strong filter coffee

Soak the raisins in 50ml Marsala for at least 1 hour.

Put the cream, milk and vanilla pod in a pan and bring up to a simmer for
5 minutes.

Meanwhile, whisk together the egg yolks and sugar until pale and doubled in
size (4–5 minutes). To temper the eggs, pour a small amount of the hot cream
and milk mixture into the whisked eggs. Then pour this egg mixture back into
the pan of hot milk and cream. Simmer on a low heat, stirring continuously for
5–6 minutes until the mixture has thickened and it coats the back of a spoon
without dripping off. Take care not to overheat the mixture and scramble the
eggs. Add the Marsala and strain the mixture through a fine sieve into a chilled
container (ideally set over ice) and cool and chill as quickly as possible.

Churn the ice cream in an ice-cream maker, following the manufacturer's
guidelines. In the meantime, strain the raisins and squeeze out any excess
liquid (this prevents the ice cream from going frosty) and fold them into the
churned ice cream. This will keep in the freezer for 2 days.

Serve in ice-cream bowls, with a shot of espresso poured over each portion –
plus a little bit more chilled Marsala if you're feeling fruity!

Honeycomb and stem ginger ice cream

Use high-quality fresh egg yolks for ice cream.

Serves 6

For the honeycomb
70g glucose syrup
40g honey
200g caster sugar
2½ tablespoons water
1 tablespoon bicarbonate of soda

For the ice-cream base
370ml double cream
300ml milk
1 vanilla pod, split in half lengthways
8 free-range or organic egg yolks
120g caster sugar
2 tablespoons finely chopped stem ginger, preferably organic

To make the honeycomb, first lay parchment paper on a large baking tray. In a large pan on a low heat, heat all the ingredients except the bicarbonate of soda. Once the sugar has dissolved and all has melded together, turn the heat up to high. When the mixture turns dark golden take it off the heat, add the bicarb and stir very quickly. It will become extremely effervescent; at this point pour it on to the tray and allow to set. Break up into small pieces of about ½cm.

Put the cream, milk and vanilla pod in a pan and bring up to a simmer for 5 minutes. Meanwhile, whisk together the egg yolks and sugar until pale and doubled in size (4–5 minutes). To temper the eggs, pour a small amount of the hot cream and milk mixture into the whisked eggs. Then pour this egg mixture back into the pan of hot milk and cream. Simmer on a low heat, stirring continuously for 5–6 minutes until the mixture has thickened and it coats the back of a spoon without dripping off. Take care not to overheat the mixture and scramble the eggs. Strain the mixture through a fine sieve into a chilled container (ideally set over ice) and cool and chill as quickly as possible.

Churn the ice cream in an ice-cream maker, following the manufacturer's guidelines. When it's ready, spoon half of the ice cream into a container. Add a layer of ginger, then a layer of honeycomb. Follow with the remaining ice cream and add another layer of ginger then of honeycomb. This will keep in the freezer for up to 2 days.

Chocolate ice cream

Use high-quality fresh egg yolks for ice cream.

Serves 6

225ml milk
525ml double cream
180g dark chocolate (70% cocoa solids), divided into two lots of 90g
8 free-range or organic egg yolks
180g caster sugar

Put the milk and cream in a pan on a medium heat until it reaches a simmer, then add half of the chocolate and stir until melted.

Meanwhile, whisk together the egg yolks and sugar until pale and doubled in size (4–5 minutes). To temper the eggs, pour a small amount of the hot cream and milk mixture into the whisked eggs. Then pour this egg mixture back into the pan of hot milk and cream. Simmer on a low heat, stirring continuously for 5–6 minutes until the mixture has thickened and it coats the back of a spoon without dripping off. Take care not to overheat the mixture and scramble the eggs. Remove from the heat, add the remaining chocolate and stir until melted.

Strain the mixture through a fine sieve into a chilled container (ideally set over ice) and cool and chill as quickly as possible.

Churn the ice cream in an ice-cream maker, following the manufacturer's guidelines. Store in the freezer for up to 5 days.

Hazelnut ice cream

Use high-quality fresh egg yolks for ice cream.

Serves 6

150g shelled hazelnuts
335ml milk
370ml double cream
8 free-range or organic egg yolks
130g caster sugar

Preheat the oven to 180°C/gas mark 4. Spread the hazelnuts on a baking tray and roast for 6–8 minutes until golden, then immediately tip out of the tray and leave to cool. Grind two-thirds (100g) of the hazelnuts finely, then separately grind the remaining hazelnuts coarsely.

Put the milk and cream in a saucepan on a medium heat, bring to a simmer, add the finely ground hazelnuts and take off the heat. Leave to infuse at room temperature for 2 hours or ideally overnight.

Strain the hazelnuts through a sieve over a pan to catch the infused cream, squeezing the hazelnut pulp with the back of a ladle to extract as much flavour as possible. Discard the hazelnut pulp.

Heat the hazelnut-infused cream in a pan over a medium heat and bring up to a simmer.

Meanwhile, whisk together the egg yolks and sugar until pale and doubled in size (4–5 minutes). To temper the eggs, pour a small amount of the hot cream and milk mixture into the whisked eggs. Then pour this egg mixture back into the pan of hot milk and cream. Simmer on a low heat, stirring continuously for 5–6 minutes until the mixture has thickened and it coats the back of a spoon without dripping off. Take care not to overheat the mixture and scramble the eggs.

Pour into a chilled container (ideally set over ice) and cool and chill as quickly as possible.

Churn the ice cream in an ice-cream maker, following the manufacturer's guidelines. Fold in the remaining hazelnuts and store in the freezer for up to 3 days.

Salted caramel ice cream

Use high-quality fresh egg yolks for ice cream.

Serves 6

335ml double cream
175ml milk
8 free-range or organic egg yolks
120g caster sugar
1 teaspoon Maldon sea salt

For the caramel
120g caster sugar
100ml warm water

Put the cream and milk in a pan, bring up to a simmer on a low to medium heat and simmer for 5 minutes.

Meanwhile, whisk together the egg yolks and sugar until pale and doubled in size (4–5 minutes). To temper the eggs, pour a small amount of the hot cream and milk mixture into the whisked eggs. Then pour this egg mixture back into the pan of hot milk and cream. Simmer on a low heat, stirring continuously for 5–6 minutes until the mixture has thickened and it coats the back of a spoon without dripping off. Take care not to overheat the mixture and scramble the eggs. Strain the mixture through a fine sieve into a chilled container (ideally set over ice) and cool and chill as quickly as possible.

To make the caramel, put the sugar in a non-stick saucepan, set it on a medium heat and melt for about 5 minutes until dark brown. When it starts to bubble, take it off the heat and stir with a heat-resistant spoon to bring the temperature down. Very slowly and carefully add the warm water (the spitting has the potential to be dangerous) and stir continuously. Leave to cool.

Whisk the cooled caramel into the ice-cream base, along with the salt. Churn the ice cream in an ice-cream maker, following the manufacturer's guidelines. Keeps perfectly well for up to 4 days in the freezer.

Blood orange

Juice your oranges; it depends on how juicy your oranges are, but 15–20 oranges tend to do it, or 1 litre fresh blood orange juice.

Transfer the juice into a relatively flat container, freeze it, and every hour or so rake it with a fork so it forms tiny little crystals (no lumps!).

Cherry (or cherry cola)

De-stone 1kg ripe cherries then whizz in a food processor and pass through a sieve.

Transfer the juice into a relatively flat container, freeze it, and every hour or so rake it with a fork so it forms tiny little crystals (no lumps!).

Add a splash of cola before freezing if you want to go for an '80s vibe!

White peach and Prosecco

Serves 6

1kg white peaches
Prosecco, to serve

For the sugar syrup
800ml water
200ml white wine
100g caster sugar
1 vanilla pod, split in half lengthways and seeds scraped out

Combine the sugar syrup ingredients in a saucepan and bring up to the boil. Turn down to a simmer, add the peaches, and cook for 5 minutes. Take off the heat and allow the peaches to cool in the liquid.

Take the peaches out and pinch the skins off, then return the skins to the peachy liquid. Transfer the skinned peaches to a dish and store in the fridge.

Put the liquid and peach skins back on a high heat and reduce to about 500ml. Take off the heat and allow to cool. When cool, transfer the juice into a relatively flat container, freeze it, and every hour or so rake it with a fork so it forms tiny little crystals (no lumps!).

Once it has frozen and is ready to serve, spoon into bowls, place a peach on top and pour a dash of cold Prosecco over the top.

Index

Index

Thank you

There are a lot of people who have helped shape this book in one way or another and I feel blessed to have you all in my life.

I want to thank all my family with whom I've spent a lifetime laughing – mostly sat around a kitchen table. Especially Ma and Matt who created a happy nest for us.

All the team at Square Peg for taking a leap of faith with this book in the first place and supporting me throughout the ride; especially Rowan Yapp.

The testers who took the time to trial the recipes at home and gave me crucial feedback, particularly Sarah Rivera.

A huge thank you to Jamie Oliver for giving me a chance many moons ago and for your constant support, especially at different stages on this book.

Thank you Nigel Slater, Sam and Sam Clarke and Anna Jones for saying kind words – it means a lot coming from such talent.

Fergus and Margot Henderson: I love you both so much and I treasure our times together. Fergus, I can't quite get over your foreword; it's the best bit of the book!

All the incredible chefs, front of house and booze people of the London restaurant scene who make this city as delicious as it is – it's a constant treat to dine here.

Thanks to our community in Islington for supporting their neighbourhood restaurant and being a jolly bunch.

All the wonderful team at Trullo past and present, you do a remarkable job and work tirelessly to create a special restaurant. I feel so much gratitude towards you, especially Sam James our superstar general manager.

To the immensely talented Conor Gadd, my dear friend and head chef at Trullo – your support and love is constantly felt.

Thanks to our suppliers who help source us with literally any product we could wish for, care as much as we do and work just as hard.

Sophie Missing, you're a wonderful human being. Thank you for helping me find the right words and putting them into sentences that made sense! You gave me confidence within myself to write and I'll be forever grateful for that.

Felicity Blunt – knowing you're in my corner always gives me reassurance and your positivity is infectious. I love that behind your kind smile is a hard-arse who will always get what's best for me! I'm glad you're on my side and look forward to our journey ahead.

Mark Evans. The man whose Jedi design skills bound this whole book together, and the only one of us who keeps his shit together! Thank you for your effort and for making this book so beautiful. You're a seriously talented man and I'll be forever grateful to you for your dedication – the force is strong in you!

Elena Heatherwick, what a beautiful soul you have. It's been memorising at times to see how you capture the world through your lens. What an honour to have you photograph my book, you've done such an exquisite job. Thank you for holding my hand every step of the way. You and your family always have a table at Timmy's kitchen.

Gemma Bell and your tribe, thank you for spreading the word and bigging us up in all the right areas to all the right people. If you're after restaurant PR, there is no one better.

Lisa Helmanis and Dada Stileman, thank for giving our restaurant spaces character and making them so beautiful.

Daisy Bird, thank you for putting up with me. You've been so supportive, encouraging and God damn useful on this book! Love you.

Jonny and Av's, thank for your incredible support and advice on so many levels. Your love and general loveliness is always felt. Also, thank you for letting me use your home to capture those wonderful images.

Teddy and Isabella, you've brought so much love and light to my life and so many people's lives at Trullo. Thank you for being little rays of sunshine.

Alanna, you believed in Trullo before it was born! You're an integral part of the success of Trullo and without you none of this would have been possible. Aside from that, you're family to me and I love you.

And finally Jordy. Standing shoulder to shoulder with you over the years has been one of the greatest rides of my life, thank you for all of it. You're a constant source of inspiration and vision for us, and man you make me laugh! I feel very lucky to have such a brilliant business partner who I also have as a best friend. What an adventure it's been!

Onwards and upwards.....

trullo

1 3 5 7 9 10 8 6 4 2

Square Peg, an imprint of Vintage,
20 Vauxhall Bridge Road,
London SW1V 2SA

Square Peg is part of the Penguin Random House group of companies whose
addresses can be found at global.penguinrandomhouse.com.

 Penguin
Random House
UK

First published by Square Peg in 2017

Penguin.co.uk/vintage

A CIP catalogue record for this book is available from the British Library

ISBN 9781910931134

Design by High-low.studio
Photography by Elena Heatherwick
Prop styling by Anna Wilkins

Colour origination by Born
Printed and bound in China by C&C Offset Printing Co Ltd

Penguin Random House is committed to a sustainable future for our business, our
readers and our planet. This book is made from Forest Stewardship Council®
certified paper.